THE BEST THING ABOUT YOU IS YOU!

Anupam Kher

HAY HOUSE

HAY HOUSE INDIA

Australia • Canada • Hong Kong • India
South Africa • United Kingdom • United States

Hay House Publishers (India) Pvt. Ltd.
Muskaan Complex, Plot No.3, B-2 Vasant Kunj, New Delhi-110 070, India
Hay House Inc., PO Box 5100, Carlsbad, CA 92018-5100, USA
Hay House UK, Ltd., 292-B Kensal Rd., London W10 5BE, UK
Hay House Australia Pty Ltd., 18/36 Ralph St., Alexandria NSW 2015, Australia
Hay House SA (Pty) Ltd., PO Box 990, Witkoppen 2068, South Africa
Hay House Publishing, Ltd., 17/F, One Hysan Ave., Causeway Bay, Hong Kong
Email: contact@hayhouse.co.in

First reprint 2012
Second reprint 2012
Third reprint 2012
Fourth reprint 2012
Fifth reprint 2012
Sixth reprint 2012
Seventh reprint 2012
Eighth reprint 2012
Ninth reprint 2012
Tenth reprint 2012

Photographs in chapters 14-25, 27-31, 34, 35 by Noni Chawla; photographs in chapters 2, 32, 38, 40-47 by Ashok Chopra; photographs in chapters 3-13, 37 by Taarini Chopra; photographs in chapters 1, 26, 33, 36, 39, postscript, acknowledgements by Raghav Khattar; photograph in chapter 5 by Jesse Robertson; photographs in chapters 48, 49, 50 by Prem Kumar Singh.

Designed by Aeshna Roy at Hay House India
ISBN 9789381431177

Printed and bound at
Thomson Press (India) Ltd., Faridabad

To
my grandfather

Pandit Amar Nath

who taught me
Bheega hua aadmi baarish se nahin darta.
(A man who is drenched is not afraid of the rain.)

Contents

Preface

As an actor with over 450 films in my repertoire, it has been my privilege to travel the world and meet several hundreds of people engaged in a wide spectrum of endeavours: From presidents to commoners; from billionaires to paupers. For me, this is not a privilege to be taken lightly as I enjoy meeting people. I also find it a very stimulating exercise to analyse them.

Actually, I find that I have a gift of analysing people. As I talk to them, I sometimes wonder what kind of lives they must be leading, what kinds of backgrounds they come from, the families they have raised and what makes them tick. Certainly, my calling as a trained actor has helped hone this process as understanding your character and getting under his skin make your portrayal more convincing.

But for me, it has not stopped at analysing others. I have constantly tried to analyse myself and reinvent myself. You cannot be emoting the same way as, say, a father, in 50 films. You have to be different and reinvent yourself. And that process begins only when you rediscover yourself.

That process of rediscovery for me began when I was contemplating my one-man play *Kuchh Bhi Ho Sakta Hai* (anything can happen) some years ago. Here I was, a very successful actor if you count the number of films I had done. And judging from the critical acclaim and the awards that I have won, I was not doing too bad a job of it either.

For a boy who had grown up in the family of a lower division clerk in Shimla with dreams for company, I had achieved fame and fortune beyond my wildest imagination. And then, like it happens to most of us, the dreams got the better of me. I thought I had the Midas touch and nothing could go wrong. As was the fashion a decade ago, I too set up a huge production house to make 'software' for the industry.

Initially, I had the most successful television programmes in my kitty. Not satisfied, I diversified even further. I went into event management, for that was the latest business to be in during those days, and staged many mega-events.

The cookie crumbled as it had to. Soon, with so many productions and events, and poor financial management, which is the bane of our business, the cash flow went kaput. And I was fighting a flurry of court cases from creditors. That was when I discovered myself and began to do some self-therapy. I asked myself:

- Why did I want to become larger than life?
- What was I in pursuit of? Wealth or happiness? Or just a larger headline than my rival production company?

In the process, I discovered many truths. And I formulated many exercises, which I introduced in my acting school called 'Actor Prepares'. (I started this school in 2005 in Mumbai.) Today, 'Actor Prepares' is also running in Chandigarh, Ahmedabad and London. It teaches people to discover themselves.

That was how I formulated *The Change Within* concept. In this volume I discuss some facets of this life-coaching programme. The purpose of my writing this small book is to initiate change – for the better – in our lives.

Anupam Kher

I

We Are All Unhappy

There is much talk of shopping endlessly to uplift your mood; retail therapy is the new phrase. Or the new world of cosmetic enhancement to give you magically good looks. Sadly, the highs of these therapies get dissipated in a short while leaving you as depressed as you were initially.

In his classic work *Anna Karenina*, the great Russian mystic and novelist Leo Tolstoy writes: '… every unhappy family is unhappy in its own way.' Yes, it is a truism that no one is happy. We are all unhappy, but in varying degrees. The seeming roots of our unhappiness stem from many perceived failings: failed relationships; failure to have offspring; failure to have enough resources; and lack of good looks. There could be a million reasons.

You would have noticed that I have used the word 'perceived'. That is because these attributes are not really our failings. We perceive them as failings from the standpoint of others. I will touch upon the effects of such a perception later. Here I wish to discuss the underlying and widely held belief that having enough money would vaporize all our failures. Unfortunately, this is not so.

It is not that Bill Gates and Warren Buffet are the happiest persons on this planet. Gates and Buffet may not lose sleep over where their next meal will come from, but like other mortals, they too are plagued with concerns about their children, personal relationships and numerous other matters. They are also worried stiff about protecting their monumental reputations. Because when you are number one in your field, there is no place else to go. You have to keep fighting all the time just to stay in place, where you are, with a pack of rivals working overtime to overtake you. Closer home, I'm sure it's the same with Ratan Tata or with Mukesh Ambani and his younger brother Anil.

I recall that way back in the 1980s the listings of the richest people on the planet was routinely topped by the Sultan of Brunei, Hassanal Bolkiah. Even today the web is replete with pictures of his gold-plated Boeing 747, his gilded 1178-room palace and the largest collection of luxury and high-performance cars.

But the main question is: Is he happy? No. His brother Jefri Bolkiah gypped him of 15 billion dollars, and many more billions were lost in bad business deals by the brother until the Sultan finally disowned him.

You would say that the Sultan of Brunei was an exceptional case.

So, let me give you a personal example. From a penniless wannabe actor, I have gone on to become a sensation earning more money than I could imagine, let alone spend. Then again, during the peak of my career, I almost became bankrupt. And I can tell you that money did not entail happiness.

That is why the retinue of people who seek darshan of the spiritual masters always has the rich and famous among them. So, money, or great wealth, is certainly not the route to happiness, as readers of John Steinbeck's classic novella *The Pearl* – described as a critique of the American Dream – have long discovered.

If money is not the answer, so too are the things that it can buy to give you an artificial feel-good feeling. There is much talk of shopping endlessly to uplift your mood; retail therapy is the new phrase. Or the new world of cosmetic enhancement to give you magically good looks. Sadly, the highs of these therapies get dissipated in a short while leaving you as depressed as you were initially.

We are beginning to realize that happiness cannot come solely from external sources. First of all we have to discover the concepts of Knowing Yourself and Being Yourself.

2

Know Thyself, Be Thyself

A little bit of introspection
will take you a long way on the road to self-discovery.
Once the process starts, you will start finding the answers
to most of your problems, instead of feeling persecuted.

WE MAY NOT AIM TO ACTIVELY PURSUE HAPPINESS, BUT WE ALL wish to minimize the unhappiness in our lives. And as we do so, we will notice, naturally, that our happiness quotient increases.

How do we minimize, if not eliminate, unhappiness? All roads lead to Rome, goes an old saying indicating that there are several paths to the same goal. It is the same with reducing unhappiness in our lives, depending on what vexes us the most.

But whatever the formulation, the fundamental issue, as old as the philosophy of Socrates, is to firstly KNOW THYSELF. This may be an old Greek aphorism, but its relevance is eternal. In a sense, we are what we are because we don't know who we are.

It is not unusual to meet youngsters who, in their late teens, are still confused about their career choices. Or young people wondering who among their friends of the opposite sex they should settle down with. Why does this happen? Because they are very unsure. They don't really know themselves.

It is even more fashionable abroad for people to wander around and 'discover' themselves. Many come to India in search of complicated new truths, but the truths are simple as much as eternal. Such as KNOW THYSELF.

I have seen many people go through a lifetime of anger, exploding at the rottenness of our society, at the inefficiency of our infrastructure, at the enormous corruption all around in every sphere of life, at the hopelessness of our political system, the callous things they are not quite capable of – or happy – doing. They have been influenced by their parents or peers. Others take up careers, or worse, marry, because they still don't know themselves or they are simply too meek to know better. The end result is a lifetime of unhappiness.

So if there are triggers in your life that make you unhappy, start reviewing yourself right now. Sit down in a quiet corner, in solitude, and tote up what makes you unhappy. Mentally place a mirror before yourself and then list all attributes – honestly – which could be contributory factors that lead on to that unhappiness.

Is your teenaged son giving you angst with his low grades? Maybe you have been at him all these months, so he is protesting subtly at your overbearing ways. Take him out for a coffee and try talking to him, and not talking down at him the next time, and see if it makes a difference.

Is your boss never satisfied with you? What triggers it off? Could it be your sloppy work or your failure to deliver on time? THINK!

A little bit of introspection will take you a long way on the road to self-discovery. Once the process starts, you will start finding the answers to most of your problems, instead of feeling persecuted. And then, after you Know Thyself, get ready for the next step: Be Thyself.

There is an old saying: 'If there is no anguish in our lives, we create it.' Yes, I have often noticed that many of us inflict unhappiness on ourselves by trying to be, or behave like, someone else. Or acting in accordance with how we *think* successful people behave. Such modified behaviour stems essentially from low self-esteem; from the belief that we are inferior beings while some others are superior to us.

There is nothing wrong in trying to emulate the good and positive points of others. Indeed, that is a very positive attribute as it shows that we are acknowledging that we are not perfect. It is definitely a more welcome state to be in than what many tend to believe – that they are perfect and all the flaws lie with others! However, there is a limit to being influenced by the attitudes of others or what we perceive to be prototypes of model behaviour.

When I say that we are trying to be another person, it is not just speaking with an affected accent or speaking a hip language or living out a 'cool' lifestyle that is indicative of the malaise. It goes much deeper and basically entails the attempt to the adoption of a new personality altogether to conform to our notions of what we ought to be.

So, we put on a mask. For example, initially, we put on one at the office to be like the boss. Then we put on many masks for the multiple roles we play. One for the spouse, another for the children, and yet another for the neighbours. Soon the mask takes over and we know not who we actually are.

I am reminded of the immortal line in French playwright Jean Anouilh's classic play *Becket* in which Thomas Becket tells a courtier who is as fixed as a weather cock: 'When your head stops turning, I hope your face will be in front!' Therein lies the seed of unhappiness, because no matter how hard we try, we will one day get tired of our revolving heads.

Let me illustrate with examples. The higher one goes in the corporate echelon, the more firm is the belief is that we must be restrained and never smile. Smiling is supposed to indicate a frivolity; the ideal is to maintain a graveyard expression as if the woes of the corporation rest on us. For example, in all the business class flights which I have flown, I have only seen my co-fliers looking and acting stiff, all wearing pinstripes, all reading the financial papers, never smiling and barely aware of their fellow passengers. And just as the plane lands in, say, Delhi, one of them will fold his papers and give you a weak smile and ask: 'Are you going to Delhi?'

If only he would just be himself and smile and be pleasant? And if everyone did so? The cabin will certainly be a much sunnier place.

3

The Anger Syndrome

... count backwards from fifty. It makes the rational part of your brain override the irrational as you are forced to break your stream of anger and concentrate on the numbers.

As I mentioned in the Preface, the purpose of my writing this small book is to initiate change – for the better – in our lives. And the only way forward is to recognize our deficiencies and seek solutions. In the previous chapter, I touched on the aspect that afflicts some of us who, perhaps from a feeling of low self-esteem, aspire to be someone else. In this chapter I would like to discuss another major problem afflicting a very very large number of people today: anger.

We all know, and hence I would not like to repeat here, what havoc anger wreaks on our physiological systems: from high blood pressure (BP) to strokes to coronary diseases. And yet an immensely large number of people today are prone to bouts of anger.

How does one fight the anger syndrome? There are many ways that have been listed elsewhere, from taking a deep breath to counting till ten to meditation. All of them have their virtues, but the problems still persist. So what does one do?

Let us tackle this subject scientifically. Check your breath when you are in a normal state. You will notice that your breath is steady and rhythmic. Now observe yourself when you start losing your cool. You will notice that your breathing gets shallow and your breath comes in short gasps. So, one obvious key to fight the onslaught of oncoming anger is to resort to deep breathing and prevent shallow breathing.

You will say that there is nothing new in this mantra. But the key is to breathe not into our chest, as we all do. The correct technique, which has been mastered by our yogis thousands of years ago and is taught in yoga schools even today, is to breathe deeply into our stomach!

In our Western-oriented society, we have become a civilization of 'shallow' breathers. As we were taught in our PT (physical training) class in school, the correct posture is 'chest out, stomach in'. Consequently, we use only the middle and upper portion of our lungs when we breathe. Now listen to what the experts say. According to James Gordon of the Center for Mind/Body Medicine in Washington D.C.: 'When you bring air down into the lower portion of the lungs, where oxygen exchange is [the] most efficient, everything changes.

Heart rate slows, blood pressure decreases, muscles relax, anxiety ceases and the mind calms.'

Gordon is not alone in this thinking. There are a host of Western researchers who endorse his views and are finding remarkable virtues in the correct technique of deep breathing.

And if you have further doubts, let me ask you to observe a baby breathe and you will see his or her belly go up and down, just the way our bellies should!

There is another old solution, which we need to tweak a bit to fight anger. Don't count till ten, count backwards from fifty. It makes the rational part of your brain override the irrational as you are forced to break your stream of anger and concentrate on the numbers.

So, keep counting backwards and take deep breaths, the correct way, the next time you find yourself flying off the handle.

4

Discontent Is a Disease

... we can bitch, crib, moan and cavil at how much more they have. Such thoughts, unfortunately, lead to the road to materialism and disaster, as the West has discovered.

As I had mentioned in Chapter 1, we are all discontented people, with varying degrees of unhappiness. Discontentment is like a disease. It keeps getting worse if left untreated.

Of course, everyone has a multitude of reasons to be discontented. But there are many more reasons why they ought not to be so. In this lies the realization of what I call 'positive benchmarking'.

Let me explain what I mean by positive benchmarking. You can wake up any morning and feel justifiably low with the blues. Your maid has said she wants an off, your driver has called in to say he is coming late so you will be delayed for that all-important appointment with the hairdresser before meeting your friends at the kitty party, your daughter has thrown a tantrum and your husband, as it always happens, is not in town.

Or, if you are a man, you could be tense over this morning's presentation as your division's sales are nowhere on target, your driver's son is unwell so you have to drive yourself to work, your executive assistant is turning out to be a turnip as he has forgotten to prepare the slides for this evening's client meeting and you have a feeling that your purchase manager is secretly demanding kickbacks. The list goes on .... Yes, both these people have enough reasons, or so they believe, to be discontent.

But let us reflect for a moment. How many Indians have maids and drivers? How many of us have the privilege of owning cars? How many of us have well-paying, if stressful, jobs? How many of us are invited to kitty parties? The moment you ask these sorts of questions, you have the answer that will resonate in your head and bring in a certain equanimity. The inescapable truth is that you belong to a small and very privileged minority and you have very little cause to be discontent.

What have we done in the process? We have benchmarked ourselves against the teeming millions of our countrymen and women who have no electricity, no houses, who very often go to bed hungry and who have no savings for a very uncertain tomorrow.

When we think of how privileged we are, that is positive

benchmarking. Of course, we can also benchmark ourselves against our friends in posh areas such as Golf Links in New Delhi or Banjara Hills in Hyderabad or Malabar Hill in Mumbai. And we can bitch, crib, moan and cavil at how much more they have. Such thoughts, unfortunately, lead to the road to materialism and disaster, as the West has long discovered.

I would like to share with you a beautiful thought, which I came to know many years ago and which has stayed with me: I always longed for a pair of shoes, until I saw someone with no feet. The powerful imagery of this humbling thought has always stayed with me. So too is a Gandhian saying: 'There is enough for the world's needs, but not enough for the world's greed.'

Mull over these aspects and you will have the answers the next time you are discontent.

5

Analyse Yourself

We can certainly leverage our strengths and try hard at whatever we excel in, but we must not be carried away with our flattered assessment of ourselves.

YOU DON'T HAVE TO TRAVEL TOO FAR TO MEET PEOPLE WHO HAVE sad tales of how unfairly life has treated them and how they have been the victims of circumstances. In a world that chases and adores success, I guess that is to be expected.

I have met alcoholics who justify their taking to drink because their wives nagged them. But talk to their families and you hear the other half of a stereophonic recording. Matters get more complicated in fields where judgements are subjective.

Singularly, unhappiness is not confined to those who have not been successful or wealthy. I find unhappiness is a great leveller. The rich businessman finds his son is on substance abuse. The globetrotting executive finds his wife is unfaithful. The industrialist finds that his competitors are outpacing him, growing larger and faster.

To all these people, the successful and the not-too successful, the mantra is simple. Your happiness lies in your hands. In a sense, the mantra boils down to analysing what your assets are, how you can maximize them and how you can play down your weaknesses. In corporate lingo, that is called SWOT analysis, which is an abbreviation for strengths, weaknesses, opportunities and threats.

That critical assessment is not the end. It is to be benchmarked against what you wish to be. And therein lies the rub. All of us must have aspirations but the key to a modicum of contentment is to see that it is in line with our SWOT findings. We can certainly leverage our strengths and try hard at whatever we excel in, but we must not be carried away with our flattered assessment of ourselves.

If I am 5 feet 8 inches and I wish to become 6 feet, then I am creating my own unhappiness. If I have a voice like a bullfrog and I aspire to become a ghazal singer, then I am consigning myself to the bin of unhappiness. If I have mediocre looks and want to become a matinee idol, I am not sure it is the path to success unless I am blessed with outstanding histrionic ability.

My mantra may be amazingly simple – remember I told you that there are no great truths that need to be discovered – but it will help you find yourself. That is, if you are honest with yourself. If you are caught in the vortex of unhappiness, it will help you find out where you have gone wrong and how you ought to refashion yourself.

The executive and the businessman may find that their unhappiness stems from paying too little attention to their wife and family. The industrialist must decide if he wishes to become happier or get ulcers looking over his shoulder all the while. To each, the choice is his or her own.

The great temptation is to aim to be rich and famous. The cold and sober realization is that not everyone can be so. One can find happiness in becoming good teachers, jewellers, designers and lawyers as well. The sooner we get started on that road, the better.

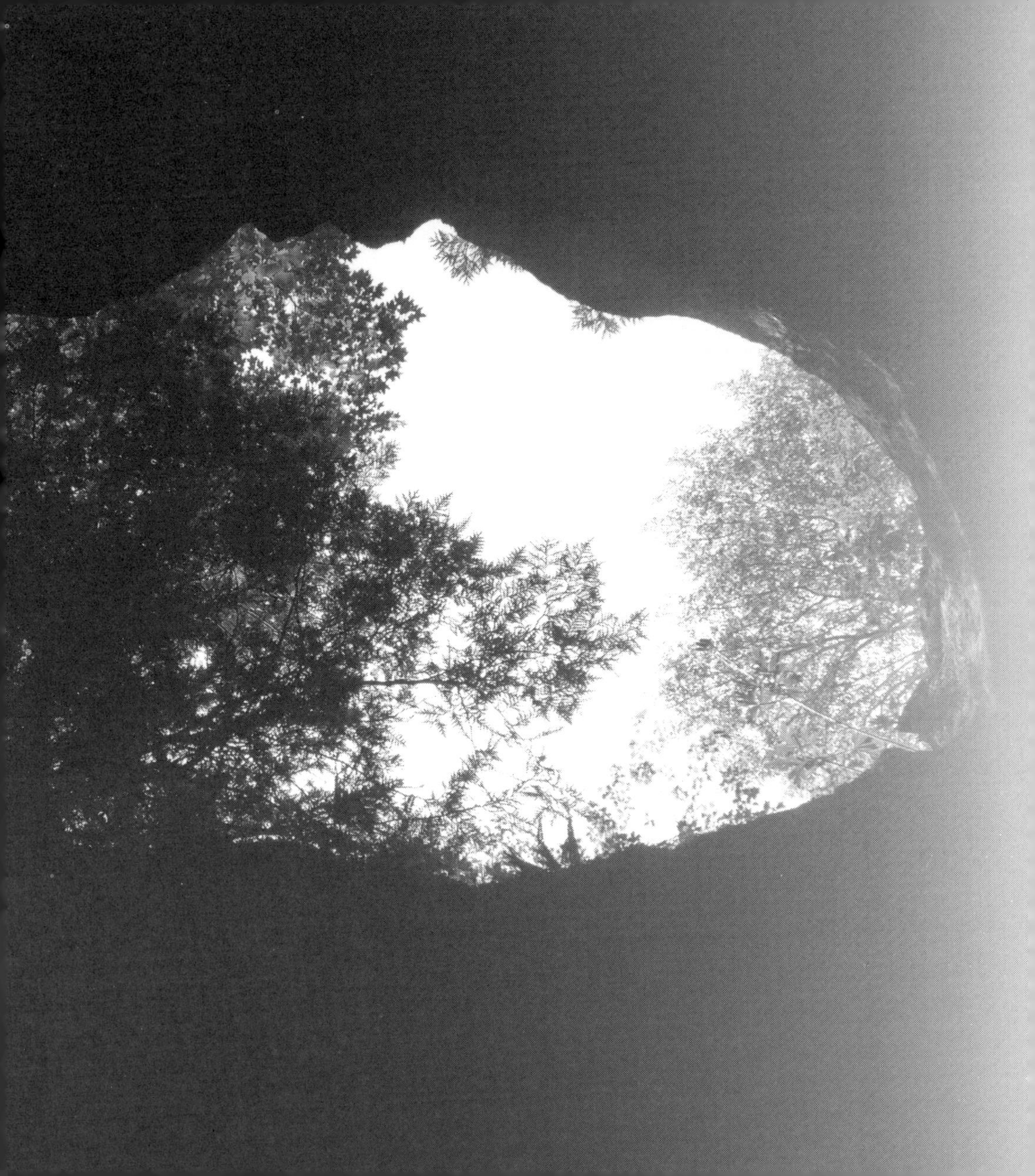

6

Comparison Begets Regret

Never read the social diary and high-life supplements of newspapers as soon as you get them as they make you feel disadvantaged early in the morning and ruin the rest of the day.

In my decades of professional life in films and theatre, I have discovered a sad truth: that most of us are driven by sadistic instincts. We like to project ourselves as being more successful than our peers and love making them feel envious of us. This attitude is the driving force behind the entire public relations business whose talents are hired by those at the top, and those vying to be at the top, of the social pyramid.

After all, what is the use of hosting a grand party if the world does not come to know of it? Such a sentiment prevails even lower down the social scale. The clerk's wife will drop it in, not too gently at all, that her husband bought her a saree costing Rs 3000 to all those she speaks with, even if sarees never were the topic of discussion. And the middle-ranking executive's wife will not tire of telling all her friends for weeks that her family has just returned from a European experience.

It is because of this innate desire in us to portray our successes, achievements and endeavours in a way that creates envy amongst those we know, that I maintain a simple rule: Meet such PR pronouncements from, let us call her Mrs X, with a smile and a stoic attitude. Do not let the statements remain with you; let them out through the other ear.

I know this is difficult, but practise it you must. Else, your inability to do so will rankle within you, make you unhappy and you will behave in exactly the way your friend/neighbour wants you to. And the scenario will be: You will tell your husband about how much of a provider Mr X is and how much of a higher wage earner he is. The implicit meaning is that Mr X is more successful than your husband. Such a message will turn into a nagging routine after a while and, finally, make your husband react one day. The explosion will leave you all unhappy; exactly how Mrs X wanted you to feel!

To make life simple and easier I have followed a simple rule, which I recommend to everyone who seeks advice: Never read the social diary and high-life supplements of newspapers as soon as you get them as they make you feel disadvantaged early in the morning and ruin the rest of your day. If you must catch up on the happenings of the bold and beautiful, and also see the ads on expensive baubles, save it for later. I can assure you that your days will pass off smoother.

Another sadistic psychological truth that you should bear in mind is that most of us are not happy if we are just better off.

To achieve complete happiness, not only must we be better off than before, but we must now be better off than the Xs who have always been lecturing us. I recall the French author and nobleman François de la Rochefoucauld's words: 'It is not enough to succeed; others must fail.'

7

Thought Control

Your life is not hopeless as there are many things that make life worth living. The point is: where do you wish to focus? On the half-empty glass or the half-full glass?

THOUGHTS ARE A DOUBLE-EDGED SWORD. THEY ARE THE foundations for the creative process and they are also the basis for turning our mindsets negative and even destructive. It is the same mind that creates the eternal art of Leonardo da Vinci, the mathematical genius of Albert Einstein and also the madness of Adolf Hitler.

It is now estimated that, on an average, 60,000 thoughts cross our minds every day. The sad part is that most of us have no control over our thoughts. One of the best attributes of a thought I have heard is that it is like mercury: you can never catch it! I think it is pretty much obvious why we should have some control over our thoughts; unless we do, we become their slave. The finest logical deduction I have read about how thoughts shape our destiny is by His Holiness the 14th Dalai Lama. He says:

> Take care of your Thoughts because they become Words.
> Take care of your Words because they will become Actions.
> Take care of your Actions because they will become Habits.
> Take care of your Habits because they will form your Character.
> Take care of your Character because it will form your Destiny.
> And your Destiny will be your Life!

I don't think there is anything more to be said on this topic after you have read, and absorbed, this simple elegant truth by one of the greatest spiritual masters of our times.

There is, however, one aspect of the thought process on which I wish to comment. It is the link between thoughts and depression, a syndrome that is endemic these days. The causes of depression are myriad but they get worsened by our recurring negative thoughts, which ensnare us.

Some of us have the ability to rationalize any untoward incident, but a large number cannot, and get sucked into depressive thoughts, which at the very worst, can virtually paralyse them. That anti-depressants are among the largest selling pharmaceuticals only reflects how rampant depression is in our rootless societies where the anchor of a joint family system has been yanked out.

So, how does one try to control thoughts? As I explained earlier, one way to control anger is to count backwards from fifty to zero.

Another method is to try to recall the happy moments of your life. Like memories of your childhood, the beautiful sunset that you last saw, the tender moments with your mother or the touch of your loved one.

It is not just enough to think of these as visuals; you should also feel these moments. If you do so, you will realize that your fit of depression is momentary. Your life is not hopeless as there are many things that make life worth living. The point is: where do you wish to focus? On the half-empty glass or the half-full glass?

8

The Phenomenon of Change

We individuals have it much easier than the world of industry as we do not have to guess at the directions of change.... All we have to do is change ourselves and go in the direction that has been shown by the wisdom of the ages.

SOME PERCEPTIONS GAIN CURRENCY BECAUSE THEY SEEM plausible. Other perceptions get accepted as facts because they have not been actively contradicted. Among them are some widely held beliefs about Change.

The concept of changing oneself seems to be redolent with a spiritual purpose. And very true, as it requires more than earthly strength to acknowledge that we have our weaknesses and need to rectify them.

However, contrary to perception, Change is neither cut from spiritual cloth alone, nor is it just an internal process nor is it always an individual's goal. Change is Big Business. And I mean not just in money terms of the revenues clocked by life-change artists. I mean that Change is more imperative to corporates everywhere than perhaps even to individuals.

Why is Change so important to corporates? Because the corporate graveyard is full of brands and companies that refused to see the writing on the wall and change. Just do a memory recall. Do you remember visiting any office that did not have a typewriter two decades ago? Now, when did you last see a typewriter in this world of computers, laptops and iPads?

The change that came in with the computer age blew out of business the typewriter giants like Remington, Smith-Corona or Olivetti. Similarly, remember the old taperecorders with spools of tape, or audio cassettes? Well, we still call them taperecorders even though they have no tape in them. The digital age made all that obsolete and sank brands like Grundig and Akai into the ground. Technology has also consigned producers of conventional televisions, ovens and phones to the dustbin of history.

Across a larger time frame, a clutch of American automobile companies have disappeared as have many legendary European watch and camera and electronic brands, thanks to the Japanese onslaught in the 1960s. Now the Japanese brands themselves are losing the battle to the Korean majors. And the world's factory is now China where everything and anything can be assembled. Such bruising billion-dollar battles for existence across nations and industries have made multinationals realize that 'If You Do Not Change, You Can Become Extinct.'

That is why Change is a multibillion dollar business of a very serious nature for corporates. And for them, unlike in the case of most individuals, failure to change will definitely be commercially fatal. What makes Change more difficult for corporates to handle is to accurately predict which parameters of their business would change. Could it be technology, or design or consumer tastes? And in which direction would the Change impetus be felt?

We individuals have it much easier than the world of industry as we do not have to guess at the directions of change. We already know the attributes that are desirable for us. All we have to do is change ourselves and go in the direction that has been shown by the wisdom of the ages.

9

Unfulfilled Relationships

Ideally, we should be able to get over these relationships, and the persons, by enveloping them with forgiveness. I think it is more important to first empathize with their point of view and only then, if we think they are right, can we forgive them.

MANY OF THE TRIGGERS OF OUR UNHAPPINESS COME FROM unfulfilled relationships. They could be ones with your parents, loved ones or friends. When relationships are unfulfilled, I find that they rankle within us and they emerge as troublesome thoughts, or dreams. Sometimes, they even become the stuff of recurrent dreams. In any case, these vexing thoughts do not leave us happy when we do a memory recall.

Why is that? It is because we all crave for a finality, a closure in every relationship.

What is closure? It is an emotional coming to terms. That is why psychiatrists say that in a flawed marriage, it is better to seek a divorce than stay on in a hurting relationship. Because a divorce is final. It is a closure to all the fights, the hurt and the crying that went with it all. Now one can move on in life.

The same logic holds for other vexed relationships as well. No one likes being dropped suddenly by a boyfriend or girlfriend. One would like to know the reason for the break-up. This is the closure we all seek.

Ideally, we should be able to get over these relationships, and the persons, by enveloping them with forgiveness. I think it is more important to first empathize with their point of view and only then, if we think they are right, can we forgive them. But how do you achieve an empathy with them? There is a powerful tool in theatre, which can aid us. We call it role-playing.

Let us assume that you are having trouble with your father over the issue of your having smashed the family car. You have of course looked at the incident from your perspective of having just one smash in the entire year. But start the role-playing exercise and put yourself in his shoes. Then ask your friend to act your role of a brash nineteen-year-old son. Let him tell you in the brazen fashion you adopt: 'Dad, I had a bang-up today.' Then act like the forty-six-year-old father and tell your friend how you had remonstrated against him driving the car that night as the roads were slippery after the rains. That you are not upset with him for the smash, but you are sad that he chose not to listen to your advice. And worse, he does not have any remorse. Your friend of course will now say that he is sick with your 'I told you so' attitude. And so it goes on …

The more you get into your father's shoes, the more you will find yourself understanding his character, emotions and thought process and the more you will start empathizing with him as you are confronted by 'your' dislikeable behaviour. If you are a girl, you could role-play your mother turning down your request for a new pair of shoes, as it is beyond the family budget.

Such role-playing helps understand situations and people. Try it and you will not be disappointed for role-playing is a very important tool in our armoury to change ourselves. It is widely used in group therapy workshops around the world and is a spin-off from the concept of Acting as Therapy.

What is the link between acting and role-playing? In a sense, every actor enacts a role. But to make that portrayal more effective, many techniques are employed, one of which is Method Acting. There are again many versions of this technique, but basically it involves the actor getting into the emotions and memories of the character. To do that, I normally recommend actors to work on a 'back story' of the character.

For example, if I am doing a scene about marital discord between husband and wife, it is important to think out what makes the man tick. I mean, get into his childhood: Was it disturbed? Was he a single child? Was he a deprived child or was he a happy child? Then what about his teens: Did he have trouble with girls or was he well adjusted? Then about his profession: Was he successful or was he unsuccessful, like the legendary Willy Loman in Arthur Miller's *Death of a Salesman*? So is he taking out his professional frustrations on his wife? And what is the nature of their discord – the fact that he refuses to change?

All these questions lead an actor to getting deeper and deeper into the skin of the character and bring the relevant emotions to the fore.

In the same way, clinically, and honestly, analyse your life – understand why you are what you are – and you will come up with the hard answers. And the person who then plays 'you' can dramatize the situations to show you how you appear to others. It is a mind-blowing experience and shows why acting can be therapeutic and also brings out the potential of role-playing.

The wonderful aspect about role-playing is that it is as applicable to obdurate teens as it is to corporate executives and is much simpler when there are groups involved. This is because it is easy to find someone to step into your shoes and act 'your' role as everyone has to be somebody else.

Among corporate executives, a majority of whom find the corporate ladder too slippery or who feel they have been short-changed by their companies, role-playing shows them their deficiencies and dramatizes exactly how they come across to their clients and bosses. Peers effectively act out the complexities of their characteristics.

I have touched upon the husband–wife interface because in my experience, it is the most troubled, and troubling, relationship of our times. Unlike in our parents' generation where gender roles were sharply demarcated, today, roles have dramatically changed. Wives are no longer always submissive. Husbands are no longer the sole breadwinners. Consequently, the issue is mostly about who wears the pants at home. Play your spouse's role tonight and you will find the answer.

10

Chasing Happiness

Remember, sadness and adversity are not to be despised or something to be afraid of; they enrich human character. They inspire us with grit and make life worth living.

EVERYBODY WANTS HAPPINESS. AND HAPPINESS, NOT WEALTH, IS the most sought-after attribute. Yet, unalloyed, complete Happiness, in the sense of an absence of Unhappiness, does not exist! This statement may seem to be a contradiction of sorts but it is not.

Taken at face value, many will wonder what is the point of pursuing Happiness if it indeed does not exist?

But be patient and you may understand the contradiction.

Many years ago, I read a legendary Italian folk tale, *The Happy Man's Shirt*, which has now also been retold by Italo Calvino. I wish to share the original version with you:

King Giphad ruled over a peaceful and powerful kingdom. His subjects worshipped him and trusted in him completely. The sun shone on his empire.

The king had a young son, Prince Jonash. Jonash, a handsome young lad graced with a strong head and many talents, lately remained in a state of deep unhappiness. Try as he might, the king simply could not understand why his son was so miserable all the time. The prince would often sit and stare out the window of his room vacantly, not at all interested in what was happening around him. At celebratory banquets and royal receptions he looked as if he'd rather be by himself in his chambers.

King Giphad could take it no longer and decided to talk to his son about what was troubling him. 'What on earth has upset you so much, Jonash? What is it that you lack? What is making you so distraught? You have not been yourself for some time now. Tell me, and I shall try and help you.'

The young prince only shrugged.

'Could it be that a damsel has caught your fancy? There are surely better ways to show your love for her than moping about the palace?'

'No, father. It's not a girl. I honestly don't know why I'm so unhappy. I feel no reason to take pleasure in anything. I want to feel better but I don't know how.'

The king could not understand this but he was certain that if this behaviour continued, Jonash would die of melancholy. Realizing that Prince Jonash now needed professional help, the king issued a decree to have his finest physicians, astrologers and wise men meet to discuss what would be the best course of action. After three days of constant meetings, the astrologers finally came up with a solution.

'Your Majesty,' Janklo, the head astrologer, spoke. 'We have given the matter much thought. In order to help our prince we must find a truly happy man; a man who is content and satisfied with his life.'

The king was slightly taken aback. 'I must find a content and happy man?'

'Yes, your majesty, and when you find the happy man you must trade the shirt he wears for your son's. All shall then be well.'

The king thought over this and finally agreed. He had notices placed all over the kingdom offering a handsome reward to anyone who could find a truly happy man. He made announcements, and sent his messengers far and wide in search of a man whose shirt would make his son feel alive again. It was not long before people started lining up to meet the king.

The first person to be shown before the king was a priest. 'Are you happy, sir?' The king's question to the priest was simple and to the point.

'Yes, majesty, I am supremely happy.'

'Well then, how would you like to become the royal bishop?' the king asked. Hearing this, the priest's face lit up. 'Of course, your majesty, nothing would bring me greater joy than to serve you!'

The king was now furious. 'Get away from my palace before I have you imprisoned!' he bellowed. 'You are a liar only looking to better himself. You are obviously not truly content or happy. Get out of my castle!'

The search continued but in vain. After two weeks, there was news of a neighbouring king who was described as an exceptionally happy person. He had a beautiful wife and many children. He had no enemies and a peaceful but powerful kingdom. Thinking that this might be the answer to his prayers, the king sent his ambassador to inquire after him.

'Tell King Giphad that it is indeed true that I have all I could ever want. My only worry is that I will die soon and lose it all. I'm afraid this very thought worries me so much that it keeps me awake at night.' With this answer the ambassador knew there was no point in taking the king's shirt home. King Giphad was disappointed and frustrated. He had no clue what to do next. His son was the very picture of sorrow and there was nothing the king could do to help him until he found that shirt.

In an attempt to clear his head, the king decided to go hunting. In the fields, he shot at a hare he saw a few metres away. The arrow only grazed the startled hare, and it fled into the woods. In trying to chase the hare down, the king moved far away from the rest of the hunting party. After a few minutes he decided to give up looking for the hare and return to the others but something stopped him in his tracks. There was a peculiar sound coming from his left. As he drew closer to the sound, the king realized it was nothing more than someone whistling. Before him in the reeds lay a handsome blonde youth. The lad lay on his back gazing up at passing clouds in the sky.

'You there! Young lad! How would you like to be appointed to the highest position in the land as the king's personal advisor?' the king asked.

'Me? An advisor?' the youth sat up and scratched his chin. 'It's such a troublesome position. I'd rather not. I'm fine enough as I am.'

The king beamed at hearing this. 'You're the one! A truly happy man at last, thank heavens! Quick, on your feet, boy.' The king took the youth back to his men. 'My son is saved! There is hope for my son yet!' He turned to the young man and said warmly: 'You may have from me whatever you wish, young man. But I need something from you as well.'

The youth looked at the king strangely. 'Please take whatever it is you need from me, your majesty.'

'My son, Prince Jonash, is dying and only you can save him. If I make him wear your shirt he could be saved. Come closer.'

The king held the youth, smiling his brightest smile and made a move to unbutton his shirt, then suddenly stopped. His arms drooped to his sides.

The happy man wore no shirt.

So, the moral of the story is that the king realized that it would not be possible to get real Happiness from someone else. Looking at the young man before him, one whose life was so different to his son's, he saw that true contentment and Happiness had to come from within, and it had nothing to do with the wealth one possessed.

He finally knew how he could help his son feel better.

Our life too ought to be like that. We must understand that Happiness cannot lie in having everything, but in being happy with whatever we have. We have discussed earlier that material wealth is not inclusive of Happiness, but the current argument goes beyond. The point that I wish to make here is that a happy person is the one who is happy even in Unhappiness. There is a wrong notion that Happiness means an absence of Unhappiness. I believe that if life serves you a lemon, make lemonade. It is only when you can accept Unhappiness as unequivocally as you accept Happiness, then you have transcended them both.

Remember, sadness and adversity are not to be despised or something to be afraid of; they enrich human character. They inspire us with grit and make life worth living. Of all the days I can recall, I can never forget the 20-odd days I had to spend in a railway platform in Mumbai when all my creditors shut their door in my face.

Here, I would like to quote from the memorable farewell speech of President Richard Nixon, who was pushed out of the most powerful office on earth (in August 1974) by the Watergate scandal. When he was leaving the White House ignominiously, he said on national television:

> Only if you have been in the deepest valley, can you ever know how magnificent it is to be on the highest mountain.

II

Be Detached

By not expecting anything in return,
we are whittling away any potential unhappiness.
That is the noblest and the most clear example to emulate.

A COUPLE OF YEARS BACK, I WAS IN THE LAKE DISTRICT IN NORTH-west England being interviewed by the BBC. It was conducted across two days, not in an indoor studio but as we rambled along the most picturesque part of the famed British countryside. For those of you steeped in literary knowledge, you may recall that this part of England was home to the Romantic poets Percy Shelley, William Wordsworth and Samuel Coleridge, who are the best remembered of the lot.

I had much time on my hands and I began responding to the question that is most often asked: 'If one is not to solely pursue Happiness, what should be one's attitude in life?'

In a sense, I did try to touch upon that point in the previous chapter by stating that we should be happy even in unhappiness. But perhaps that answer was too simplistic and philosophic.

In plain terms, I think the concept is to try to be like the mystics: be unmoved by experiences whether happy or sad. It is akin to the state of being an official observer at a diplomatic event. He just observes. He does not participate in, or get moved by, the proceedings.

We get moved by emotions because we allow ourselves to participate and get enmeshed by happenings. We must become like true mystics who transcend all feelings, Love or Hatred, Happiness or Unhappiness. In short, we must become detached.

Many will recognize in this concept the essence of Buddhism, and indeed of many Indian faiths such as Hinduism and Jainism, which also dwell on the virtues of such a detached view of life.

Apart from attachment, it is also unfulfilled expectations that trigger much Unhappiness. So, on another plane, we can place ourselves in the role of a *karmayogi* in which we work without any thoughts about the benefits from our actions. We should do our work well because that is our karma, and not for any special recognition. We should similarly do good deeds, not for any gratitude but because that is the way it ought to be. By not expecting anything in return, we are whittling away any potential unhappiness. That is the noblest and the most clear example to emulate.

Here I am reminded of the legendary inspirational poem 'If' written in 1895 by the Mumbai-born Nobel laureate British poet-storyteller Rudyard Kipling, which first appeared in his collection of short stories and poems under the title *Rewards and Fairies* in 1909. The poem is inspirational, motivational, and provides a set of rules for 'grown-up' living. It contains mottos and maxims for life, and is a blueprint for personal integrity, behaviour and self-development. I strongly feel that 'If' is perhaps even more relevant in today's karmic times, than when Kipling wrote it, as an ethos and a personal philosophy. No wonder lines from the poem appear over the players' entrance to Wimbledon's Centre Court – a poignant reflection of its timeless and inspiring quality.

I would like to conclude this chapter with a few lines from 'If'. But before I do that, let me mention here that the beauty and elegance of 'If' contrast starkly with Rudyard Kipling's largely tragic and unhappy life. He was starved of love and attention and sent away by his parents; beaten and abused by his foster mother; and a failure at a public school, which sought to develop qualities that were completely alien to Kipling. In later life, the deaths of two of his children also affected Kipling deeply.

If you can dream – and not make dreams your master,
If you can think – and not make thoughts your aim;
If you can meet with Triumph and Disaster
And treat those two impostors just the same …
If you can fill the unforgiving minute
With sixty seconds' worth of distance run,
Yours is the Earth and everything that's in it,
And – which is more – you'll be a Man, my son!

12

Relive and Relearn

It is time that we realized that our reactions are game-changers for better or worse. They can make our life; or they can mar it. That is why I believe that our Destiny is often in our own hands.

I REALIZED MANY SUMMERS AGO THAT THE WAY YOU REACT CAN often shape the outcome of events.

Few of us understand this fact and most of us go blithely through life carrying on as we have always done; never reliving or relearning from our actions. And our acts also affect our Destiny in the long run.

It is memorable that I am writing this chapter on 19 June – a day that is being celebrated as Father's Day. I would like to relate an incident involving my father, which taught me a lot about action and reaction.

I come from, what I would like to call, a low middle-class family. My father was a Himachal Pradesh government servant based in Shimla. His income would hardly make both ends meet for the family with the result that an outing for a meal in a restaurant was quite a rarity.

Being in government service, he had access to the secondary school results a day or two in advance. I was not a bright student. Hence, when two days before the matriculation results were to be announced, my father invited me to a restaurant, I was extremely curious what the occasion was all about. After feasting on kachoris and samosas, and still wondering over the reason for the feast, my father said: 'Son, I have to give you some sad news; you have failed in your matriculation exams ...'

I have learnt many things from my father, but the most memorable of them all was this one incident when he did not condemn my failure. Instead, he handled it superbly and with care. In today's scenario, when you hear of so many tragedies over failure on the declaration of results, I truly realize the extraordinary emotional quotient of my father. I don't think any other parent would have handled that situation like him. Even today, I think few parents will have the same attitude as my father.

Decades have passed since that incident. And today, I find a similar approach detailed as the 90:10 Principle by one of the most famous management thinkers, Stephen Covey, the author of the international bestseller *The Seven Habits of Highly Effective People* published in 1989. Basically, he states that 10 per cent of life is made up of what happens to you; 90 per cent of life is decided by how you react.

Covey illustrates his Principle with an example of how you can react if your daughter spills coffee on your shirt as you are leaving the house for work. One scenario: You shout at your daughter (and she breaks into tears!); you shout at your wife for keeping the coffee mug too close to the edge; both of you get into an argument; you change your shirt hurriedly and then rush through – forgetting your briefcase – and the cop halts you for speeding, fines you and delays you . . . and so it goes on through the day.

You could have another scenario: You could tell your daughter to be more careful the next time, change your shirt unhurriedly and pick up your briefcase on the way out and drive away peacefully!

Both the scenarios began the same way but they ended dramatically differently. Why? Because of your reaction.

It is time we realized that our reactions are game-changers for better or worse. They can make our life; or they can mar it. That is why I believe that our Destiny is often in our own hands.

13

Live Now and Forget the Past

'Life is not about surviving the storm,
it's about dancing in the rain.' In living each moment,
we should experience sadness in sad times
and happiness in happy times.

MOST OF YOU WOULD PERHAPS REMEMBER THE LYRICS OF THE legendary Urdu poet and Hindi film lyricist, Sahir Ludhianvi, sung by Mohammad Rafi for Dev Anand's evergreen film *Hum Dono* (1961):

Main zindagi ka saath nibhata chala gaya;
Har fiqr ko duaen mein udata chala gaya ...
(I went along with the flow of life;
I blew away every worry in a puff of smoke ...)

One of the main causes of unhappiness is that most of us choose to dwell, or daydream, about the past or the future. We do not wish to live in the present and leverage the most from it. We largely tend to look back on incidents that shaped our lives, most of them in a negative way, and constantly say to ourselves: 'What if it had happened this way?'

If we are not romanticizing the past, we are trying to blame others for the way things eventually happened. I have come across so many people who have failed to accept the past; whether it is in terms of broken relationships or lost fortunes. Unfortunately, none of them could do much about their present because their past always intruded. Depression finds an easy dwelling in the minds of such people. And then things go downhill.

Please remember that the past cannot be changed and the future is uncertain. All that we have is the present. And it is the present that can help us change the future. So, the point of it all is to make the most of every moment that is available to us by applying ourselves in a focused manner in the present time.

And how does one achieve such concentration? By meditation. I have briefly written about meditation in Chapter 15, but I have not elaborated as there is enough literature available.

Yet, the one aspect that escapes many of us is that meditation is not just a calming exercise to be practised in sessions. Meditation is essentially about being conscious of every action that we perform in our every wakeful moment. In other words, meditation is about living the moment.

One of the finest sayings I have heard, and whose origin has not been established, goes: 'Life is not about surviving the storm, it's about dancing in the rain.' In living each moment, we should experience sadness in sad times and happiness in happy times.

Living is not about trying to escape any experience; it is to live through it. For example, we cannot escape childhood and rush to adulthood; it is important to be a child and live through fears, animosities and, yes, daydreams. I can tell you from experience that child celebrities who have not had a normal childhood have always felt that they lost out on their innocent years.

So if you are writing, as I am at this moment, immerse yourself in writing. If you are dancing, lose yourself in the dance. And if it is raining, as it might during the monsoon season, go out and enjoy the rain. Live and enjoy each moment as if it was your last. There is an adage in English that if you look after the pennies, the pounds will look after themselves. In a similar vein, I believe that if we look after the moments, our lifetime will look after itself.

To quote Og Mandino (from the USA), one of the most widely read inspirational and self-help authors in the world, who has provided hope to those struggling with life's challenges:

> Live this day as if it will be your last. Remember that you will only find 'tomorrow' on the calendars of fools. Forget yesterday's defeats and ignore the problems of tomorrow. This is it. Doomsday. All you have. Make it the best day of your year. The saddest words you can ever utter are: 'If I had my life to live over again.' Take the baton, now. Run with it! This is your day!

14

Contemplation Helps Us Understand Ourselves

'Last night I dreamt I was a butterfly.
How do I know that now I am not a butterfly dreaming that I am a man?'
The conundrum in this alarmingly simple question stumps me.

On a quiet morning, when the nation was in bandh mode, I went along an interesting stream of thought. I believe it was Albert Einstein who said that the simplest questions have the toughest answers. My thoughts went out to the genius when I was adding a new wrinkle to the eternal metaphysical question: Who am I?

I came across an interesting response, which said: 'I am a collection of memories.' Indeed, it was a very unusual interpretation to the age-old question, because in every sense, we are our memories.

You realize the implication of this thought only when you see senility in the elderly. The man or the woman is the same person physically, but what is the person in reality when he or she does not even remember who he or she is? Such people are not even allowed to sign legal documents; so who are they?

There is another wrinkle to this version of reality. It is very beautifully explained in the context of the caterpillar and the butterfly, which I notice is a favoured symbolism of Buddhist philosophers: 'Just because the butterfly does not remember that she was a caterpillar, does it mean that she was not a caterpillar?'

Similarly, we often wonder if we too were ever infants. We have no memories of the days when we crawled on all fours and took our first stumbling steps. Hence, we have to rely on our elders, and photographs, to understand that we indeed were toddlers once.

There is a further philosophical reference, a brilliant one, to the butterfly, which takes the breath out of the 'who am I' question. It is a Japanese Haiku (poem), which says: 'Last night I dreamt I was a butterfly. How do I know that now I am not a butterfly dreaming that I am a man?' The conundrum in this alarmingly simple question stumps me.

The point of going back to the original question once in a while is that it is a humbling thought and it brings us closer to ground reality. In essence, we all don different avatars through the day.

As a parent, as a spouse, as a son or daughter to our parents, as a staffer in office, or as a person in society, we effortlessly flit in and out of these personalities. But sometimes there is a grinding of gears. We take out our anger, suppressed on the work front, on our children. Or we unleash our troubles with our teenaged children on our helpless and aged parents. It is during these times that we would do well to ponder: Who am I, really?

It is a precursor to a more detailed review we should have every week; a sort of audit of our actions, which will help us come on track. The Catholic clergy do it annually by retiring to a retreat. We too could profit from such periodic contemplation. It could help tell us who we really are.

15

Motivation Is the Key

... our minds are so devilishly wandersome
that they need to be focused on the mantra
all the time to remain pure.

IT IS TIME TO LOOK BACK AND CONTEMPLATE.

In the previous chapters we have discussed myriad issues on subjects such as: Who am I? Know thyself, be thyself; chasing happiness; and role-playing.

But the keynote of all such initiatives is to keep practising till they become part of our mental matrix. If we have relationship issues, we should seek out – and practise – the relevant guidelines we have discussed. We must keep at it till the positives we are trying to achieve get ingrained in our DNA so that the negatives do not recur. I know that many people who undergo self-improvement programmes give up because practising a new regimen gets tiresome as motivation levels flag after a while.

Which is why, it is common for people to ask for personal coaches in fitness gyms. But personal issues are different and not amenable to such coaching. How do you know when you will have an explosive fit with your son or daughter for your personal coach to be around?

So the key, I maintain, lies in constant practice. No one has learnt swimming, or tennis, or cycling – or any activity – merely by reading textbooks. You have to get on the ground, or the water, and practise regularly to master the discipline.

When I was in my teens, I used to constantly wonder why monks, and many elderly people, chanted mantras for long hours. After all, I thought, if they were so spiritual then a few hours of chanting should suffice. Many years later I understood that our minds are so devilishly wandersome that they need to be focused on the mantra all the time to remain pure.

The situation can be well illustrated through an example doing the rounds on email. A young novitiate was asked by his master to meditate for many hours at a stretch. One day, when they were on the banks of a river, the young monk asked the elder in an irritated manner what was the earthly benefit of repeated meditation. The elder smiled and asked the boy to pick up a wicker basket left on the sands by fishermen, run to the water, collect some in it and bring it to him to drink. The youth was stupefied: 'How can I bring water in a basket full of holes?' The monk asked him to try. At first try, the youth brought back a few drops. 'Run faster', advised his master.

Many attempts later, the youth managed to get barely half a scoop and was wondering what the exercise had to do with his question. 'Observe,' said the elder monk. 'You may not have collected enough water for me to drink. But have you seen how clean the dirty basket has become because of your constantly dipping it in the river?'

I think you get the moral of the story!

16

Destroy the Ego

... my cardinal rule to everyone is: Never take yourself seriously. We all develop egos because we acquire a very serious image of ourselves as we grow older and we do not like to be made fun of.

THE BIGGEST STUMBLING BLOCK WE FACE IN THE GOAL TO SELF-realization is the ego.

Ego feeds on itself and grows as we meet with success in the material sense. It manifests itself when we are not prepared to see the other person's point of view and then admit our fault.

We like to think that we are always correct. In our belief, it reduces our stature if we admit our mistake. Such an attitude is not necessarily attached to success. Parents have ego problems with their children and seniors with their juniors. And I may be criticized here, but in the Asian way of life, it is normally husbands who have very large egos vis-à-vis their wives.

As a parent, how many times have you admitted to your child that you may have been wrong in rebuking him or her? As an older sibling, how many times have you apologized to your younger brother or sister for having been unfair with him or her? Not many times, I am sure. There is no cure for this attitude except to follow the dictum of every wise man: Destroy the ego.

There are many ways to gradually de-emphasize your ego. Many group therapy classes abound, in which participants criticize your behaviour, habits, attitudes and so on, in a bid to sensitize you to your drawbacks. Such classes are expensive, monetarily and emotionally, and sometimes prove to be a bit too harsh to handle.

I have a much more relaxed approach to handling the ego: Add a dash of humour to the entire exercise. In my acting classes, instead of dissecting the individual, which makes him or her feel like a wet rag and resentful at the end of it, I encourage participants to make the approach very humorous. Such humour takes the sting out of the analytical process and yet gets the message across.

Apart from classroom exercises, my cardinal rule to everyone is: Never take yourself seriously. We all develop egos because we acquire a very serious image of ourselves as we grow older and we do not like to be made fun of.

Also, we are very conscious of our 'image'. However, it is this projection of the image that makes us false and stressed. We will not laugh at jokes in the midst of people we consider our social 'inferiors' because we feel it would bring us down to their level.

On the other hand, we will laugh at things we do not even understand merely because our 'superiors' laughed and we don't wish to project an image of an ignoramus.

Just observe a child: see how he or she laughs without a care in the world. He or she does not care who is watching, nor does he or she care if he or she is making a funny face. The child is laughing because he or she is living the moment and it is a genuine feeling.

Sadly, as we grow older, we are more conscious of the false values around us and we lose that spontaneity. Try and learn to laugh, as it increases your face value!

17

Learn to Laugh at Yourself Too

Humour goes beyond mere laughter; its therapeutic effects have led to the formation of laughter clubs everywhere and the fact that it is effective as a social lubricant, in dissipating tension, is undisputed.

Most of us take ourselves too seriously. Just look at those pompous politicians all around you. Even making a funny remark about them has become a dangerous matter. There are then the businessmen who are booted and suited and when did you ever see them smile? And there are their juniors who believe in emulating their bosses to move up the ladder. All in all, it is a humourless world.

Indeed, humour has not been given its weightage as a topic of serious concern, though its role has been widely appreciated in the performing arts.

Everyone has laughed during a Charlie Chaplin film and grown up with those Laurel and Hardy and Abbott and Costello comedies.

When we were children, humour was an integral part of our lives. Unfortunately, as we grow up, many of us forget the world of laughter. We erroneously believe that humour is not for grown-ups. We erroneously believe that successful people need to look grave and serious all the time.

Frivolity is a strict no-no in the corporate world, so no one wants to be a joker in the office. Sadly, all these beliefs are misplaced. Humour goes beyond mere laughter; its therapeutic effects have led to the formation of laughter clubs everywhere and the fact that it is effective as a social lubricant, in dissipating tension, is undisputed.

In every public speaking course, among the things aspiring speakers are told is to use humour in the opening sentences to ease the tension in the audience. Predictably, when the speaker makes some joke on himself, the tension evaporates. But the key here is to make fun of oneself …

I can tell you from experience, as I am among the fortunate few to have been blessed with the ability to look at the funny side of things. When things went wrong for me some years ago, I decided to make a play looking at all my setbacks in a very comic perspective. That one-man, two-hour-long play, *Kuchh Bhi Ho Sakta Hai*, has been a hit in all the countries it has been staged in and it recently crossed the 200-performances mark.

What is indeed even funnier is that it is a scream with even the serious corporate types who never smile in their offices. One corporate house after another wants me to stage a performance or two for them! Why is that so? And why should I write about humour in this book? Because it is important to see the funny side in any situation. That is how we can make light of any matter and not get stressed. I once landed at a crematorium in Delhi, wanting to be there at the last rites of a director. After some time, I realized I was at the wrong crematorium. Rather than make it obvious, I played along and saw the humour in the situation.

Many people crib and crib and crib about their problems. I think they should realize that there is a famous adage that laughter is the best medicine.

18

Unleash the Power Within

... the road to self-actualization is to address the internals and ACT. Focus your attention on the task at hand and do not give in to stray thoughts and easy options.

I HAVE COME ACROSS MANY PEOPLE WHO ARE UNDER THE impression that merely attending self-coaching classes, or sitting at the feet of a guruji, a baba or a mataji, will make them self-realized individuals. Such an impression is far removed from the truth, just as if mere recitation of prayers will make us better human beings.

The main aspect is to realize, as I have explained before, that we have to be internally awake and conscious of every action and thought of ours. And the key word is 'internal', as without that internal will, no amount of external force can make us realize the power within us.

No one who has achieved any bit of success can deny that before the external obstacles were tackled, the journey to success had to begin by fighting the internal obstacles. These could be in the form of sloth, fears, low self-esteem, distractions, temptations, worries, past failures and so on.

As I write these words, I am reminded of my own internal conflicts, which I had to overcome on the road to achieving success. I had studied in a Hindi medium school and was not proficient in English. I was already balding at 23. Coming from a family of very modest means in Shimla, I was neither acquainted with the use of cutlery nor had been exposed to fine dining experiences. One of my legs was marginally shorter than the other. I would think that such handicaps were quite a plateful for me to surmount.

But I did it.

In life, I have discovered, through analysing my experiences, that it is always the inner that shapes the outer. As someone asked me the other day – have you ever wondered over the preponderance of 'ins' in the language of self-realization? Why it is w-in and not w-out, in-trospect and not out-rospect, in-tuition and not out-tuition, in-sight and not out-sight, in-spiration and not out-spiration, in-stinct and not out-stinct? And the list goes on …

All great breakthroughs have always been from our thoughts, which are internal: Whether it was that genius Greek mathematician, physicist and astronomer Archimedes of Syracuse discovering the principle of floatation, or the English astronomer Issac Newton discovering gravity, or the Germany-born theoretical physicist Nobel laureate Albert Einstein enunciating his theory of relativity. The internals have even been the subject of our sages who understood their importance thousands of years ago.

An immense amount of current research in advanced fields such as neurosciences has only proved the existence of the power within us; that even the best of us use barely 10 per cent of our mental capacity; and that the brain rewires itself continuously and is capable of learning new things at any age.

So the road to self-actualization is to address the internals and ACT. Focus your attention on the task at hand and do not give in to stray thoughts and easy options.

You cannot learn swimming by reading a book; you have to dive into the pool. So take a dive into the pool of life. You will not merely experience the change within; you will also unleash the power within.

19

Value Yourself

... no one is superior; we are all differently abled.
Your esteem and self-worth are in your mind.
Believe that you are the best in your field
and be confident of your talent.

There is a saying that the more things change, the more they remain the same. This is especially true of human attributes and problems. If you think that we are seeing the nadir of corruption, think again. Jesus was sold for 30 pieces of silver. Licentiousness and debauchery hit a high point in Roman times. And greed was at the root of the Mahabharata.

Our problems too are ancient: Unfaithful spouses, truculent sons, tyrannical bosses, unscrupulous politicians, rapacious traders and so on. If you introspect, they haven't changed much since the days when Brutus and his group assassinated Julius Caesar.

But a few things have changed, which is to be quite expected in these days of the Internet and Facebook. And among the new fangled problems that besiege us, I find one inadequacy that is fairly common in Generation X: low self-esteem.

I think this is a syndrome of our times; a byproduct of days of plenty. During my childhood, I don't think such feelings existed. In a small town, everybody knew everyone else and his or her net worth. No one could pretend to be from a station higher than what he or she was born into. Everybody knew your salary and your bank balance and so there was no stress in trying to pretend being richer than what you were actually worth.

Low self-esteem is more pronounced in cities where most of us are rootless, faceless migrants; all the while pretending to be richer and better pedigreed than our neighbours. The pressure of competition is so intense, and the motivation to earn money so high, that people spend decades pretending that they are far better endowed financially, hold better jobs and are better educated than they actually are. They often do not know who they are till the end.

Some people, the ones with a conscience, however, get tired of the game and they lose belief in themselves. They are the ones with low self-esteem. And they are actually the more honest ones in the rat race, which they have given up, as they cannot compete with the deceit of the rat pack.

They find it too difficult to cope with the hype and hoopla of marketing strategies, which are currently required to promote themselves, be one an aspiring copywriter, a struggling actor, a budding author or even a corporate executive. It is an age in which packaging is more important that the package itself.

To such people, my advice is to pamper themselves in the physical and psychological sense and never to think that the man next to them is better. I believe no one is superior; we are all differently abled. Your esteem and self-worth are in your mind. Believe that you are the best in your field and be confident of your talent.

The best way to start is to make a list of twenty qualities in which you excel. Everybody has so many virtues; the point is to dig deep within. If you can find these positives in yourself, then can you doubt that you are a winner?

20

Spring Clean Your Life

We must travel light in the spiritual sense too.
We have to shed our anger, our ego, our falsity, our deceit – to be on the right path. By divesting all these traits, we grow closer to our true selves.

ALL OF US GO THROUGH AN ENTIRE LIFETIME COLLECTING things. I am not just talking about the collectors of pens, stamps, watches and similar objects. I am referring to common people such as you and I who live in our own houses and have a lot of clothes and accessories; much more than what we need. And along the way, we start acquiring junk. Like the kerosene stove we used two decades ago or our grandmother's handi in which we used to heat water. The point is, do we realize it?

I realize it every time I drive through the city of Mumbai, and indeed much of India, where millions of people live in shanties. I am always fascinated by the meagreness of their belongings. Their entire life's possessions can be packed in a briefcase; let alone a suitcase. Imagine them, and the vast tribe of travelling performers, mendicants, knife sharpeners and so on, who wander on our streets, in your mind.

Are they lesser mortals than you and I? It is a very good exercise to put yourself in their place, or believe you are in a spot of emergency, and imagine that you were allowed to carry just one bag. What would you stuff it with? Your wallet, your family pictures, some clothes, a toothbrush .... But certainly not your party shirts or formals. Why then do we have so many possessions? Are they genuinely required? Do they add to our happiness? Can we not cut back on our consumption levels, wherever we are on the economic ladder?

Just as it is time to take a periodic review of our material possessions, a time for spring cleaning, it is worth taking a review of our qualitative possessions as well. There is a belief in us that spiritual growth too is an acquisition. Such a belief is very far from the truth. The change we seek is actually a divestment of our base qualities. By shedding such qualities, just as we shed our possessions, we become lighter and enlightened. We must travel light in the spiritual sense too. We have to shed our anger, our ego, our falsity, our deceit – to be on the right path. By divesting all these traits, we grow closer to our true selves. We kindle and awaken what was already inside us, but which had been buried by decades of collecting the wrong baggage.

It is said that when the Buddha, on attaining enlightenment, was asked what he had attained through so much penance and meditation, his reply was: 'Nothing. I have awakened to what was already within me ...'

In the words of another enlightened soul, Swami Vivekananda: 'Awaken, arise and stop not till the goal is reached.'

21

The Wisdom in Fables

You will rediscover in them [fables] the wonderful world
of truth, honesty, bravery, integrity and innocence;
virtues we have all long since left behind,
along the journey to adulthood.

'WORDS ARE A SOURCE OF MISUNDERSTANDINGS', WROTE THE legendary French aviator-writer Antoine de Saint-Exupéry in his immortal classic *The Little Prince*, which ranks among my favourite books. This novella, which is on the list of all-time bestsellers, is supposedly a children's fable and has been translated into 190 languages and has sold over 90 million copies. Adapted to various media over the decades including stage, screen, opera and also a gripping audio rendition by Peter Ustinov (a renowned film maker, actor and dramatist), it has many profound observations about human nature, like the thought that I have just quoted.

The Little Prince makes you gaze deep into yourself as you encounter characters that are faithful replicas of the people you meet; and you discover the shallowness of them all. I am always amazed by the simplicity of the thought that words can cause misunderstandings. After all, words are there to express, communicate, clarify and resolve disputes. But whenever I hear heated arguments, I understand how the same words are also a source of conflict. This is particularly true of couples, where, in an argument, one does not often mean what one says. 'I don't want to ever see you again!' is not to be taken in the literal sense, as any number of boyfriends, lovers and husbands will attest to.

Which brings me to another Exupéryism: It is only with the heart that one can see rightly; what is essential is invisible to the eye!

Why am I talking about a fable? Because fables have a universal appeal and they address universal truths. They are not couched in esoteric jargon nor do they attempt to intellectualize a simple question and leave you, at the end, feeling foolish for having asked that question.

As I have said before, there are no great truths still waiting to be discovered. They just need to be rediscovered and lived by. We all have the truth within us, but it lies deep down, forgotten.

That is when the fables jolt us and bring the answers to the top of our consciousness. You will rediscover in them the wonderful world of truth, honesty, bravery, integrity and innocence; virtues we have all long since left behind, along the journey to adulthood.

In *The Little Prince*, the protagonist falls in love with a rose. And he is truly besotted with her as he thinks she is the only rose in the world, till he discovers fields of roses! Predictably, he is crushed. But he realizes another simple truth: People may raise five thousand roses in the same garden – and they don't find in them what they are looking for. And yet, what they are looking for could be found in one single rose!

The sad fact is that we have forgotten the fables of our childhood: Jataka Tales, the Panchatantra, Aesop's Fables, and so on. Read them once again, with feeling, and they will rekindle in you all the virtues that you are seeking.

22

Handling Familiar Blues

...flip through the pages of your life more often than you do.
You will not lose anything and the bad times
will be a passing memory too.

THERE ARE MANY DAYS WHEN WE GET THAT DOWN-IN-THE-dumps feeling, those familiar blues. A feeling that nothing is going right, that nobody cares for you. How does one handle that?

Did you know that we all have a very powerful weapon in our arsenal which we seldom use, except when we grow old. It is our bank of memories.

The memories of our happier days work as a powerful trigger to elevate our moods. If it is a work situation that causes you distress, recall the moments when you were truly happy at work. Like your promotion or like the time your boss congratulated you on a job well done.

If it is the family that is vexing you, just go into that family archive.

There are always a million things around you that can be mood elevators. If your son is obdurate, remember when he gave you a slobbery kiss and a tight hug when he passed the board exams. Or when your troublesome daughter spent days with you when you were recovering from a surgery. Or any such little little incidents.

Perhaps your memories are too dim or you are really feeling so down that you cannot recall anything nice about your friend who has been tattling about you behind your back.

Change tack and pick up an album. Nothing is as refreshing as a photographic recollection. Even if you cannot remember incidents from the recesses of your mind, a photograph jolts you without any effort.

There you are with your first missing tooth. And your first day at school when you stubbornly held on to your mother's hand. Your days in school – how soon you grew into a young man! – are all captured in the annual ritual of class photographs as you turn the pages.

Your marriage photos. And then perhaps, the pictures of your own family. Life comes full circle here, captured in light and shade. That is why the company Kodak never says it sells film; it claims to sell memories!

Who cannot be moved by such images as you take a walk through life? Even if you have that sinking feeling, such fond memories make the blues fade away and let the sunshine into our lives.

As the cat Grizabella sings the memorable song 'Memories' in the Andrew Lloyd Webber musical *Cats*:

Daylight. I must wait for the sunrise
I must think of a new life
And I mustn't give in.
When the dawn comes tonight will be a memory too
And a new day will begin.

So flip through the pages of your life more often than you do. You will not lose anything and the bad times will be a passing memory too.

23

Forgiveness Erases Bitterness

... the only way forward is to genuinely forgive those who have been unkind towards us. Such an attitude is, if you examine it dispassionately, meant for our own benefit and enhances our own peace of mind.

FORGIVENESS SOUNDS LIKE A PHILOSOPHY LOADED IN FAVOUR OF losing out in life. It also smacks of a game plan of the weak as it does not exactly reek of macho-like qualities that are so much in demand currently.

But is it really so? Not if you realize that forgiveness is a philosophy that is designed to protect us from recurring thoughts of retaliation. It is a philosophy designed to heal us from the impact of negative thoughts. We seldom realize that our thoughts govern our actions, our lives and therefore our destiny.

When we do not forgive someone who has hurt our feelings, we nurse a grudge and we long to get even. That reduces it to pure revenge which we seek. If we have the means to extract that revenge, we believe – quite wrongly – that our feelings are soothed.

But this belief is patently wrong, as revenge is never concluded; it is a vicious spiral.

Revenge soon returns when the other party retaliates and soon things get out of control until no one remembers how it all started. That is how there are family feuds that run down generations and no one can get off the mad whirligig even if they want to. The words of Mahatma Gandhi describe the logical end of such behaviour: 'An eye for an eye will soon make the world blind!'

What happens if one is not in a position to strike back? The feeling of impotent rage keeps rankling within us and, like a corrosive acid, it slowly eats into our innards. It makes us tetchy and unhappy. That is certainly not a good state of mind to be in. Hence the best solution – and the only way forward – is to genuinely forgive those who have been unkind towards us. Such an attitude is, if we examine it dispassionately, meant for our own benefit and enhances our own peace of mind.

When I advocate genuine forgiveness, I do not mean that we should hang our principle of forgiveness outside our houses for all to see, or communicate our attitude for those who have hurt us. In today's unforgiving and rough world, it would be a badge that would mark us out as easy prey. But what I do advocate is that we truly forgive them in our hearts, so that all bitterness gets erased and we bring about a 'closure' to a turbulent incident in our lives.

Only in genuine forgiveness and a 'coming to terms' can we live a richer or more meaningful life. Or, we will always be travelling with an accumulation of unwanted baggage of the past.

24

Can Love and Detachment Co-exist?

... they can. And why should they not?
It must be remembered that
detachment does not mean neglect;
it means letting things be.

LOVE MAKES THE WORLD GO ROUND, GOES AN ETERNAL ENGLISH song. Certainly love is a great motivator and all the world loves a lover. But love is also precursor to many of our problems.

To be technically correct, our problems lie not in love or the act of loving. Love is a very selfless state of being and it is one of the rare times in our lives when we are happier while giving, rather than receiving. When you love someone, you are prepared to wait for hours on end at the coffee shop or at the mall ...

But the flip side of such love lies in expectations, which arise in us over time. We start expecting – maybe loyalty, maybe understanding – from our partners and others too. Sometimes these expectations are too irrational or just get too much to handle. We expect our loved ones, our relatives, to forgive us our frailties, and when love meets with disappointments over time, it boils over.

Love also leads to attachment. And that attachment is actually a comforting illusion since all attachments will pass away and lead to a sense of loss. If there is attachment to an object, say, a painting or a rare watch, it stirs a material craving in us, then pride over the possession and finally worry – whether it would be lost or damaged over time. Most of the collectors you read about are people who are more worried than happy!

So, what is the point of their possessions? That is why all the great sages have advocated a life of detachment along the quest to spiritualism.

The moot question is: Can detachment and love co-exist? To a large extent, and in a balanced mind, they can. And why should they not? It must be remembered that detachment does not mean neglect; it means letting things be. I agree that it is easier to give up our attachments, gently, for material things. We can give up luxuries and be more basic in our wants. However, the true test lies in detaching ourselves from our near and dear ones.

We can start by not interfering in their decisions and by lowering our expectations from them.

We can then focus on spending our time for larger and more general causes, such as education and poverty reduction.

Gradually, we can give a new focus to our lives, one that is slightly removed from family and friends.

You may say that this is easier for those who have the means to be independent, but you will be amazed at the number of people from humble abodes who strive ceaselessly for social causes.

Ironically, if you observe, the solution for getting out of this love/attachment syndrome is just another version of the same. It is in giving unto others rather than ourselves, just like lovers, that we will get redemption.

25

Old Wisdom from New-Age Gurus

... in all times of uncertainty throughout history,
we all seek the same old wisdom but from new-age gurus.
That is why we need 'The Change Within' and
the life-coaching books in the stores.

A FEW WEEKS BACK, ON ENTERING A BOOKSHOP, I WAS STRUCK BY an ever-rising trend I have found in all bookshops these days. There are not just shelves, but entire sections, devoted to books chalking out programmes to deal with the problems of life. These sections are commonly known as Mind, Body, Spirit.

Decades ago when I was a student, there were self-help books like Dale Carnegie's *How to Win Friends and Influence People*, Thomas A. Harris' *I'm OK, You're OK*, and E. F. Schumacher's *Small Is Beautiful*. Then came books on subjects such as yoga and meditation, which were normally the choice of those in their fifties. A decade or so ago, spiritualism became the new fashionable norm and authors like Louise Hay, Deepak Chopra, Wayne Dyer and Brian Weiss became the rage. Then we all gorged on the Chicken Soup series. Now, there is a younger audience out there and there are the new icons, in authors like Paulo Coelho, Robin Sharma, Jim Stovall, Rhonda Byrne and numerous others.

Why are we seeing such a surge of interest in self-help books in our country at a time when all our economic indices are at historic highs and India is the second-fastest growing economy in the world?

The answer lies therein – that we as humans are unable to cope with such growth.

Underlying such a blistering pace of growth is the bewildering array of choices before us in every product field, due to which our lives have become complex.

We have forgotten that until just about 20 years back, we had a choice of two cars. Today, we can choose from almost 400 car models with prices ranging from Rs 1.4 lakh for the Nano to Rs 4.5 crore for a Rolls Royce coupé. From just one reputed cosmetic brand, we today have access to over fifty brands at the last count. The product lines have exploded.

Similarly, in education, where we once aspired to be in the IITs (Indian Institutes of Technology) and IIMs (Indian Institutes of Management), the current generation has the world to choose from and thinks nothing of planning for a career in MIT (Massachusetts

Institute of Technology) or at the Kellogg School of Management, both in the USA.

Life has become even more complicated when it comes to financial decisions. A decade ago, we just had the Life Insurance Corporation with a clutch of policies. Today we have many companies with over a hundred complicated insurance schemes. And there are even more complex investment choices in place of fixed deposits, mutual funds, debt instruments, derivatives, commodity options and so on.

My belief may be slightly controversial, but to look at it my way, every major economy had time to ingest the growth process. Not India. The US and Europe have had television since the 1950s and have seen it grow to colour to cable to satellite in the 60 years since. We have compressed all that into just about two decades.

Such hurtling change has reworked our attitudes, our culture, our expectations and our DNA, leaving our traditions imperilled and making us all feel a little dazed. In such times, as in all times of uncertainty throughout history, we all seek the same old wisdom but from new-age gurus. That is why we need 'The Change Within' and the life-coaching books in the stores.

26

Discard Excess Baggage

You need to discard excess baggage from the suitcase of your mind. All that baggage of retribution, all those bitter memories, anxieties and negative thoughts need to be jettisoned.

SOME OF THE MOST GROUND-BREAKING THEORIES IN PHYSICS HAVE emerged from what are called thought-experiments. Contrary to perception, such work did not involve massive banks of computers or huge laboratories. They involved just simple but profound thoughts and the goal was to explore the potential consequences of the principle in question. Most of Albert Einstein's work was based on such thought-experiments, of which the most famous occurred at the age of 16.

Young Einstein thought he was riding a beam of light and the consequent observations later led him to formulate his famed theory of special relativity. But what do the frontiers of theoretical physics have to do with 'The Change Within'? Plenty!

A year or so ago, I lectured on 'The Change Within' programme at some of the famed management institutes in the US – among which was the prestigious Kellogg School of Management. I was, and still am, struck by the enthusiastic response to such a non-traditional subject among those who ingest balance sheets and marketing strategies faster than I can devour an idli.

Here, a thought-experiment strikes me: what would you carry if you had to evacuate your house in an emergency and all you were allowed was one stuffed suitcase?

Your cheque book? Your insurance policy? Your diamonds? Your wads of cash? Your prayer books? Your photo albums? Obviously, some clothes would find a place in that suitcase. But the rest of the stuffing would determine what kind of person you are. Quite right, some affluent people would agonize over the kind of clothes they would carry: should it be formals or party wear or simply casuals? How should they be presenting themselves in front of the media glare when they run out of their homes?

The ones with more modest incomes and homes would find that their choices may have been automatically made. They do not have such a vast collection of personal trappings.

What comes next? The affluent would naturally opt to cart their wealth with them and a suitcase might not be sufficient. In any case, there is nothing much in which they place much value, except Mammon.

The not-so-rich might think of carrying at least an album full of memories; what is a life fully lived without memories, anyway?

The sensitive souls might include at least a book that they may have found meaningful. The spiritual might include a prayer book. And the sportsperson might carry a hockey stick or cricket bat … it could come in handy in an emergency after all!

Our minds too are such a suitcase. You need to decide every once in a while what you should carry and what you should discard. You need to discard excess baggage from the suitcase of your mind. All that baggage of retribution, all those bitter memories, anxieties and negative thoughts need to be jettisoned. And just as in the hypothetical suitcase, your mind's contents will also reveal what kind of a personality type you are.

Think of more such thought-experiments. They will give you a badly needed reality check every once in a while.

27

Friends Make Life Better

I for one strongly feel that it is important to maintain friends.
Friends help us destress.
They help us connect with the world outside.

In the crush of modern urban life, there are many things that we have lost long ago. Some of these cannot be retrieved; like making food the way our mothers made or getting our clothes stitched and not picking them off the racks. Yet one loss that has physiological and emotional costs is the art of making friends and maintaining friendships.

I still remember the friends who used to come to our home in Shimla; they were the salt-of-the-earth types. They were people of humble origins, but of integrity. People who had links with my family for decades, if not generations. You could relax with them and be yourself. There was no need to put on airs or show off your latest acquisition. They were the types our family could turn to in times of need or crises; and considering our humble origins, such times were quite a few.

As I look back and ponder, that community feeling is now very tenuous and frayed. Even the friends that are there can be counted on one's fingers, unlike in the case of my father, who has friends everywhere.

Why is this happening in times when we have the most modern telecom facilities ever? Why is it that we still cannot connect with friends who are in the same geographic area as we are, but we connect with yet others on the other side of the earth through the new social networking sites?

We all know the answers. They are lack of time and lack of opportunities, but more importantly, lack of will coupled with ambition. We now make friends only with those we wish to know and we jettison them as soon as they are no longer useful. One look at your old diaries and collection of visiting cards can tell you the story.

I for one strongly feel that it is important to maintain friends. Friends help us destress. They help us connect with the world outside.

It is sad that in a majority of cases, particularly in cities and towns, our friends are drawn from our list of peers and office colleagues. What does that reduce us to in our spare time? Chatting with colleagues about office affairs even on holidays? Working up your bile again on how so and so got the better of you at that meeting?

For women, the need for connecting with gal pals is even more imperative, as studies have shown that women need much more nurturing and care and comfort than their men can offer. It has been proven that sisterhood is necessary as women understand and empathize better with other women, wherever they may be. Yes, gossiping is indeed good for women, it has been proven.

So take out that old directory and call up that friend you have not met since college. As you talk of days gone by, you will laugh at the old jokes of your professors and your blood pressure is bound to come down.

And be grateful that you still have such friends to phone up.

28

Confront Fear and Fight It Off

The problem with our fears is that
we always hide behind them;
and that attitude makes our fears larger than they really are.

All of us have fears. There is no one in the world who is without them. Indeed, to fear is to be mortal.

The rich eternally fear whether their investments will grow faster than the rate of inflation and whether their children will manage their legacies well. The middle class, in turn, fears sickness and the lower classes fear poverty. The farmer fears a failed monsoon. The actor fears a box-office flop. And the politician fears the verdict of the electorate.

Many polls have been routinely conducted by news magazines and news organizations to find out what people fear the most. And an interesting fact that has emerged is that different nationalities fear different things. Fears of old age, of being broke, of being left alone, are universal, but their ranking changes across nations.

Old age has been traditionally feared in Western nations, where youth is the eternal dazzler. All ad campaigns, TV shows and products are youth-oriented and the senior citizens feel marginalized as if they did not exist in public consciousness. Hence, in the US and Europe, the money spent on anti-ageing products and therapies is staggering.

In Asian countries, which accord respect to grey hair, it is normal to see the elderly in the public eye. But with growing urbanization and increasing dependence on children, old age is creeping up the fear charts.

I too had fears and I was mortally afraid of failure. After my first film *Saraansh* (1984), I met with a kind of success that I had never dreamt of. But fate teaches us all a lesson. I turned entrepreneur and I had several business reverses, which virtually wiped out my net worth. That was truly frightening. I worked out my fears by writing and acting in my autobiographical play *Kuchh Bhi Ho Sakta Hai*, which continues to be a resounding hit even today. It was a public performance of all the failures in my life; from my first romance to my business reversals. I was a changed man after that first night's performance. Figuratively, I stood naked before the audience and now I had nothing to fear.

Not all people can stage a play about their lives. But some do write about their experiences and yet others publish their thinly veiled tales as fiction. Such a letting out of emotions gives people immense relief. You too should adopt that open-air policy and speak openly to your friends and colleagues about your fears. They will reduce in course of time and may seem to be even farcical later. The problem with our fears is that we always hide behind them, and that attitude makes our fears larger than they really are.

Another approach is to rationalize our fear with the question: Is that the worst thing that could happen to me? Let me illustrate: Suppose you are afraid of committing yourself to marriage, or you fear going bald. Is that the worst thing that could happen to you? Certainly not! You could get bankrupt or you could die a painful death. In comparison, your fears simply pale into insignificance.

So fear not, you have nothing to fear but fear itself!

29

Don't Allow Inhibitions to Limit You

You will understand how to handle yourself and your emotions when you are in front of people.
You will learn how to be confident and at ease in an assembly.
This is a very powerful exercise.

THE WORD INHIBITION IS A VERY LOADED TERM REPLETE WITH varied imagery. To some it may connote something very mild, such as speaking in public. To others, it may connote things much more adventurous, such as streaking in public. Whatever be the benchmark, there is nobody I have met who does not have inhibitions.

In a very broad sense, inhibitions limit our behavioural norms. And that can be a good thing, or a bad thing, depending on how we feel. In a way, inhibitions reflect – and are a function of – our public morals and are not a negative aspect. Many of us do not lie or cheat because we are not comfortable doing so; so we are inhibited in that sense. But there are many other inhibitions that negatively impact our behaviour and leave us wishing we could overcome the sense of shame or fear that we attach to them.

I think fear and shame are very limiting inhibitions. Both are intrinsically connected to acts, which we wish to perform, but cannot. Like the inability to cogently argue in public, or the fear of acting on stage, or the shame of making mistakes or giving wrong answers. All these are aspects of a deficient personality, which millions wish to overcome, but cannot.

How should we overcome such limiting inhibitions? Frankly, it is easier said than done if one is alone and it is much easier to deal with the issue in groups.

For starters, if you are alone, stand before a mirror. That is your group. Make the funniest faces you can and laugh at yourself. Loosen up and see how soon you are comfortable with yourself.

Next, emote a story that you have heard, which has really moved you. Act that story out in first person; as if you are narrating it with all you have to a confidant. With practice, by enacting different stories, you will come to terms with yourself and your persona.

You will understand how to handle yourself and your emotions when you are in front of people. You will learn how to be confident and at ease in an assembly. This is a very powerful exercise. Remember that even the legendary orator, who stirred a nation to fight great odds heroically, constantly practised his speeches before a mirror. I am referring to the former British prime minister, Winston Churchill, who led England to victory against Adolf Hitler in the Second World War.

In groups, it is easier to open up. Let each one talk of the one time he or she became a laughing stock, of the stupidest mistakes he or she ever committed, of the first crush, of one incident he or she regrets and so on. Soon the group will gel as one. And you will see the strength come into each one of them and the fear of speaking out, or being themselves, evaporates.

The point to remember about inhibitions is that practice makes them disappear!

30

Don't Fear Change

I know many well-placed executives who have quit their cushy corporate jobs and turned teachers, farmers, consultants, become entrepreneurs or written books or joined NGOs or even started film and theatre production companies.

We are all creatures of comfort and security. Given half a chance, we would all like to live in our cocoons all our lives. But change we must, for that is the order of life.

The first change comes when we leave our schools and go to college. We move out of our circle of friends with whom we had grown up for over a decade. We have to make new acquaintances and adjust to the new environs. The next change comes when we seek professional employment; the routine is repeated once again.

Finally, we settle down in our vocations and then we coast along. Though this seems to be an ideal situation to be in, it is actually fraught with stagnation and slow death. There is a name for this affliction – mid-life crisis.

Not unusually, this syndrome affects more men than women since the latter are more linked with change given their strong bonding with family and children. Many men do the same routine in their jobs and stop learning, and soon discover that their younger colleagues are brighter and faster. And they cannot accept it.

Their spouses are no longer without an opinion; they have grown in the decades and are now independent, emboldened women. And the husbands cannot tolerate it. They find their children are no longer in their control; the children are already in their professions and do not need their fathers for advice. The fathers cannot understand it.

The only cure for all this is to flow with the tide and constantly reinvent oneself. Corporates recognize this syndrome so they have management-education programmes with fancy names. Tired executives attend such programmes in salubrious surroundings and return reinvigorated, spouting fresh jargon to impress their juniors.

For the others who do not have sponsors, the need is to rediscover and re-evaluate themselves through life-coaching programmes, find a new challenge and then realign their energies. The more intrepid recognize the ennui creeping up on them and quit their jobs altogether and take up another assignment in an unrelated area.

I know many well-placed executives who have quit their cushy corporate jobs and turned teachers, farmers, consultants, become entrepreneurs or written books or joined NGOs or even started film and theatre production companies. I know doctors and lawyers who now get greater satisfaction in working for charities than making more money.

The critical point is to find a new challenge. Take up photography and you will be absorbed in the world of light and shade and colours. Or learn a new language like French or German. Or join a dance class or an acting workshop. All such activities have the potential to refashion your personality.

So the mantra is to not fume when your coping mechanisms fail and the world is passing you by. Stop the bus and get off. Take a vacation with your better half and discover yourself. And find a new challenge …

31

Children Need Grandparents

... my friends do not have the time to carry on with the great tradition of oral storytelling of our country. Their children have the latest electronic gizmos but – for no fault of theirs – they have no value benchmarks, nor do they have any heroes worth emulating.

EVERYONE WOULD AGREE THAT OUR CHILDREN ARE THE MOST precious gifts we have ever received, or will receive, in our lives. Indeed, children alter our lives even before they are born. In many homes, parents yearn for them, plan for them and dream about them even before they enter this world.

And from the moment they are born, they take over our lives. Ironically, despite all our yearning and love for them, they also have the potential of turning into our biggest nightmares later in life.

What goes wrong?

It is not an easy question to answer on a general basis, particularly since circumstances are different from home to home. No one can generalize and say that the fault lies entirely with either the children or the parents. But one thing that I strongly believe in is a universal truth that in our desire to give our children what we did not get as children, we do not give them what we got as children.

Once the veracity of this statement sinks in, you will find many instances in homes across the land and across the socio-economic spectrum that bear it out. When I was a child, my grandmother narrated the great epics to my brother and me; she also instilled in us the values and morals of the heroes.

My case was not exceptional. The situation was the same in all my friends' houses as well.

My grandfather too used to tell us children a lot of pithy sayings, none of which I have forgotten. Among the most memorable is this one, which I have recalled many times during the dark phases of my life: A man who is drenched can never be afraid of the rain.

I do not see many such 'growing up' scenarios in the homes of my friends these days. Their children, who are in homes many times more affluent than the one I grew up in, very often do not have the benign influence of grandparents since these are modern nuclear families. Neither do my friends have the time to carry on with the great tradition of oral storytelling of our country. Their children have the latest electronic gizmos but – for no fault of theirs – they have no value benchmarks, nor do they have any heroes worth emulating.

The scene is not too different in the home of my help. There, television has killed the tradition of storytelling and economic compulsion has made the parents work longer hours away from home, thereby giving them less time to be with their most precious assets.

I am talking here of just one instance, which I am sensitive about, particularly since it is established that the first six years of a child's life are the most critical to his or her emotional psyche. There are innumerable others, which I am sure you can spot if you analyse the situation. So, think about your childhood and give your children elements from it while you still can. Else, you will eternally regret your inaction.

32

Hope beneath the Wings

It is difficult to say what is impossible,
for the dream of yesterday is the hope of today
and the reality of tomorrow.

Hope is not just another four-letter word. It is perhaps, together with Love, the most powerful emotion known to us. If Love makes the world go round, Hope keeps us going on forever. Even in the worst of times, it is Hope that keeps us alive. Hope makes us believe in a better tomorrow and it is Hope that gives us the courage to face all odds. As it is said, when Hope is lost, all is lost.

Why am I writing about Hope in this book? For several reasons.

Because there can be no better times than festivals to kindle Hope in all of us through friends and families. It is a time when estranged friends make up and it is the season when the son or daughter, who had drifted apart, could be making that long-awaited reappearance.

Truly, there is Hope in the air …

There are many places that abound in Hope. There are places where there is a dire need for such a strong emotion. I have seen it in the eyes of patients with life-threatening ailments. I have seen it in the eyes of relatives of patients imploring surgeons to dig out the cancers in their loved ones. I have seen it in the eyes of victims of starvation and I have seen it in the eyes of believers praying fervently before deities asking for a wish to be fulfilled.

Sometimes, we mix up dreaming with hoping. Both are aspirational, but dreaming can be extended to a fantasy. As children we all dream to be various versions of Superman. Hope is, however, largely rooted in reality and the possible.

We hope to do things that are in the realms of what is achievable. Yet to be honest, there can be no clear segmentation as, sometimes, dreams do come true! In my own case, I could never have dreamt to be as successful an actor as what I have become!

If I have seen Hope, I have also seen Despair. And that is tragic because I have been witness to many talented people gradually giving up on Life, Living and finally Hope itself.

I'm sure all of us know of such people and it is gut-wrenching to be around them because, ultimately, the strength to live must come from within. Not from someone else. The creative arts are home to many of them, and they embody the phrase that Hope never abandons us; we abandon Hope.

So, when we are sometimes caught up in the vortex of thoughts such as: I am not good looking, so I cannot win her; I cannot get that job as I cannot do a good presentation; or I will never be able to complete my studies as I do not have finances, think of Hope.

And think of this memorable quotation:

It is difficult to say what is impossible, for the dream of yesterday is the hope of today and the reality of tomorrow.

33

A Good Story Can Change Our Lives

... if you know any noteworthy story
worth being relayed to a larger audience,
tell a media person. Or tell me.
A good story has the potential to change our lives.

NEVER HIDE YOUR LIGHT UNDER A BUSHEL, GOES A FAMOUS biblical saying. The light referred to here means your talent. Indeed, from biblical times, you do find many people who do not believe in shouting about themselves and their accomplishments from rooftops. They believe that their work should speak for itself. That indeed has been the hallmark of the true greats for they never hired town criers to advertise their talents or products.

Can you imagine William Shakespeare advertising his plays? Or Wolfgang Amadeus Mozart his compositions? Or the Dutch post-Impressionist painter Vincent van Gogh his art? Or Learnado da Vinci his genius? That is why, even now, the tradition of relying on word-of-mouth publicity is practised in various professions and there are strict rules refraining doctors, lawyers, accountants and others from advertising themselves.

In my case too, distrust of those who advertise too much with in-your-face campaigns persists. After all, anyone can buy advertising space. But no one can buy a reputation or product quality. Even now, there are many worthies who desist from advertising their success.

A year or so ago I was in Belgaum (in Karnataka) performing my play *Kuchh Bhi Ho Sakta Hai* at the invitation of the Karnatak Lingayat Education Society. Why did I make an arduous journey to a regional city? Because I wanted to get a close-up with a little-known society that runs 211 educational institutions, which includes colleges of medicine, dentistry, engineering, law, nursing, Ayurveda and also schools and girls' hostels.

What I saw impressed me immeasurably. Apart from the fact that its hospital had the most child-friendly children's ward I have seen anywhere, I was surprised to learn that treatment was entirely free! Even more surprising was that the society's trustees were running English-medium Central Board of Secondary Education (CBSE) schools in *talukas* (equivalent to a part of a district), thereby shattering the image of English as an elitist language and opening the doors of global opportunity to rural children.

I found my answer to the question of why the society is not well known in the rest of Karnataka, much less the rest of India. It is not interested in luring investment from non-resident Indians (NRIs) or in building state-of-the-art hospitals in the metros because it aims at uplifting millions of rural people and bringing them under the net of development. It is not even mentioning remotely, not to think of advertising, its achievements.

Over the years I have met many immensely talented people who, like the Karnatak Lingayat Education Society, are publicity-shy. Much as the media is vilified, I think it plays an important role and communicates with society at large. If positive stories are not put out, what remain are puff pieces and projections. And that is why we have been reduced to a society without icons.

Just as we have the right to seek information to keep a check on the misuse of authority, we have a right to tell a story. So if you know any noteworthy story worth being relayed to a larger audience, tell a media person. Or tell me. A good story has the potential to change our lives.

34

A Smile Can Conquer Stress

... we take a lot of crap from our bosses whom we will not look at if we move into another job. But there is very little crap we are prepared to take from the people whom we truly love. Think about it and you will realize how to overcome stress in your house at least.

MANY DECADES AGO, *TIME* MAGAZINE SET THE BALL ROLLING when it ran a cover story titled: 'STRESS – The Silent Killer'. That was years before stress became a fashionable syndrome and a word in common currency.

Today, there are many instances of people beating 'stress – the silent killer' by retiring to the mountains or taking up farming in rural communities. But taking up sanyas is not the answer to the syndrome as we all (city dwellers) have active lives to lead in urban agglomerations. So, why is stress so enduring and proving difficult to conquer?

The simple answer is that we get stressed in certain situations and, when we do so, we generate stress around us, which only multiplies. It is the cause of much unhappiness and a host of maladies ranging from diabetes to paralytic strokes in most of us today. We can get stressed out for any number of reasons: when our neighbour gets a bigger car or when his son gets better grades than ours. There can be myriad other examples: as when someone overtakes us on the road of life. The underlying factor in all such cases is the envy factor.

We cannot do anything about such events, much less control them. But we can control our reactions. And that is what I have always advocated. I would like to compare our response to a situation as if someone overtakes us when we are cruising along. We have a choice; we can either smile, or we can get flustered, exhibit road rage and press the accelerator pedal. Our reaction will determine the outcome of that moment.

It is the same in our everyday life. I see parents talking down, harshly, to their teenage children who are tired of listening to the same old lectures for the umpteenth time. So, they switch off. The result is that the parents and the children soon lose contact with each other, leading to even more stressful situations. It is the same with our spouses, our significant partners. We lecture them about their faults till we turn nags.

In all such situations, the message we aim to deliver is not incorrect; it is the manner of delivery and the reaction that are being faulted. I believe that instead of reaching out in these circumstances, we get stressed out. And then we pass on stress to our loved ones and the moment to reach out is lost forever.

In conclusion, I must say that I am always struck by the irony of one aspect in our lives: we take a lot of crap from our bosses whom we will not look at if we move into another job. But there is very little crap we are prepared to take from the people whom we truly love. Think about it and you will realize how to overcome stress in your house at least.

35

Minor Issues Obstruct Happiness

... we must realize that unless a decision is taken to address the larger picture in a mature manner, the minor irritants will continue to rankle within us and make us more unhappy.

We all acknowledge that there is nobody in this world who is always happy; all of us have reasons to be unhappy. True, some have more reasons, others have less. But unfortunately, even those with lesser reasons sometimes believe that they are the most unfortunate of us all.

What is more distressing is that, many a time, we do not know or understand the reasons for our unhappiness. If we talk to counsellors, they will tell us of couples that are breaking apart for the most trivial of reasons.

Some of the most common irritants in relationships, I understand, are of the woman getting peeved at the man constantly throwing his wet towel on the bed when he leaves home – treating it as a hotel room. At other times, the woman gets upset at the soap being squashed by the man during a bath or she considers it icky to find him leaving behind hair on the same cake of soap that she will have to use.

Lest this be construed as a case of bathroom wars, let me add here that women also get upset at men leaving toilets dirty, speaking in raised voices and in not being sensitive to their moods.

Men have much less reason to be grouchy about; they often object to the wife's fetish to keep the bathroom bone dry through the day and to her constantly keeping everything in its place so that the house looks like a page out of an ad for good homes.

I think there is no debate on the fact that these are very minor issues and that they are hardly the stuff for break-ups. The truth of the matter is that, in all these cases, there are larger issues that form the unhappy backdrop to these relationships – which I call the larger picture – but which remain unresolved. Hence the unhappiness factor erupts in these minor flare-ups.

In most instances, the unhappiness in the larger frame usually stems from intangible fundamental issues such as the wife not being treated well by her in-laws, the husband himself ill-treating her or the children, the husband not doing too well professionally or squandering his earnings on liquor and so on.

From the man's perspective, the issues might be that the woman is giving too much weightage to her parents' views in their relationship or that she might be neglecting the house. These are issues that are finding resonance across the socio-economic strata and cannot be addressed at short notice. But unless their existence is first acknowledged and then addressed, they will continue to be swept under the carpet.

The real factor is that many such issues continue to rankle and fester in us and then grow into a cancer, because we believe that we will rock the applecart of the relationship if we do some plain speaking. But we must realize that unless a decision is taken to address the larger picture in a mature manner, the minor irritants will continue to rankle within us and make us more unhappy.

36

Discover Your True Strength

... what does one do in stressful times ... when one is wrongly charged with a trespass that one did not commit? I resolved not to react as it would make matters spiral out of control.

SEVEN DAYS IN APRIL 2011 WERE REMARKABLE, WITH ME BEING ON a swing between one end of the spectrum and the other in terms of activism. What started as my participation in a non-violent crusade ended up with me being the target of violence. The period was also perhaps the stormiest I ever witnessed in decades.

But why should I write about my vicissitudes here, you might well ask, and quite rightly so. I am referring to them here as it was an acid test for me whether I could remain committed to the principles that I write about.

It all began very peacefully on 5 April 2011, with me at Jantar Mantar in New Delhi, joining the ranks of supporters of the activist

Anna Hazare in his crusade against corruption. At the rally, I was interviewed by several television channels. Some politically mischievous elements in Mumbai misrepresented my comments about the Constitution to say that I had stated that it (the Constitution) should be thrown out, or words to that effect.

My alleged comments raised the hackles of legislators in the Maharashtra Legislative Assembly and the speaker passed a privilege motion against me, calling for an investigation. No amount of replaying of my quote by the channel – in which it was clear that I never stated anything even remotely resembling what my detractors were trying to allege – could pacify the politicians that the channel interviewed.

My acting school in Mumbai was the scene of demonstrations that afternoon and, later in the evening, my apartment block was stoned. The next day, my effigies were burnt in some parts of the city. All this happened because of something that I had never said; because of something that was intentionally created by some with an ulterior motive.

Hence, what does one do in stressful times like this, when one is wrongly charged with a trespass that one did not commit? I resolved not to react as it would make matters spiral out of control. But more importantly, I did not react as I did not feel compelled to react. I did not lose my sense of calm even though I was incessantly badgered by the media for comments and bytes for several hours.

In retrospect, I was happy with the way I reacted to the tumultuous events. It is very easy to be on the sidelines and give expert advice, but the true test comes when one is facing the heat. The next morning, I went to see the gentle nun who initiated me into the world of differently abled children a decade ago, Sister Maria Dolores.

To me, she has always embodied spiritualism. After a quiet chat, she left me with a moving message, which I felt was crafted for readers of this volume: 'Remember Anupam, your fight is against corruption … and not against the corrupt. Do not confuse one for the other. Forgive those who threw stones at your house; they do not understand what they have done. In your peace will lie your strength.'

I said amen to that!

37

Accept Change, but with Wisdom and Grace

... aloneness is available today for the asking. It is this aloneness that traps you and segregates you from society. It leaves you cold and indifferent to your surroundings and it has also led to an erosion of the good old-fashioned values such as sharing and caring.

When I grew up in a large family in a small house, the underlying theme of our existence was one of sacrifice. Apart from my family circumstances, those were truly trying times for everyone and self-denial and self-abnegation were the hallmarks of family life everywhere. Parents routinely sacrificed their dreams and desires for their children and elder brothers and sisters put their ambitions on hold for their younger siblings.

There were other small things, which went with that way of life. Everything that was bought was shared around by everyone – whether it was a packet of biscuits or a bar of chocolate. The entire family would gather around one television set – or one radiogram

– and watch one programme or listen to one artiste. There was a togetherness all around in everything one did.

You did not have to be a Gandhian to lead such a simple life; such things came naturally to everyone.

But then those times were truly different. Today, value systems seem to have undergone a complete change. Youngsters everywhere are more comfortable with freely expressing their needs and desires. They do not believe in holding anything back, certainly not their wants. It is, what I call, 'the I, Me and My generation'. It is the age exemplified by the iPod and the iPad – where each person listens to his or her brand of music and is lost in the virtual world, all alone, even when in a crowd.

In contrast to my times where it was an effort to be alone, aloneness is available today for the asking. It is this aloneness that traps you and segregates you from society. It leaves you cold and indifferent to your surroundings and it has also led to an erosion of the good old-fashioned values such as sharing and caring.

There are other values that are gradually fading from our consciousness: attitudes of gentleness and civility. In these days of high-pitched marketing, the threshold of receptivity has gone down many times. Few people are patient, or have an attitude, to persevere at what they are doing and wait for the results to reflect the merit of their work.

Instead, many resort to high-pitched drum-beating to hype their rather meagre endeavours. As an artiste having worked for over a quarter century in the film industry, I see the change happening around me all the time. This is not just about complaining about a way of life that is slipping away; it is about how such changing attitudes have impacted our psyche and our approach to life.

Change is indeed a way of life; yet change must not be accepted for the sake of change. Every aspect of change need not be progressive; some aspects can be regressive. So, while changing, it is important to grasp the kernel of the matter and decide if the change is for the better or otherwise. We cannot lose out on eternal truths, values and virtues on the altar of progress. As the saying goes: 'We must hasten … but slowly.'

38

Fear Has the Ability to Numb the Senses

... the sad aspect is that in many cases, our powers of observation are compromised for long periods in normal times. That is because we choose to see only what we wish to see and choose to hear only what we want to hear.

STRANGE AS IT MAY SOUND, SOMETIMES THE EYE CANNOT REGISTER what it sees. Or the ears do not hear the sounds they listen to. There are many surprises and contradictions in our sensory perceptions, which we should understand as we grow older. For example, one would expect several eyewitness accounts of the same incident to concur on all aspects. But talk to any criminal investigator and you would be surprised at the amount of variance that emerges from such eyewitness reports when under trauma.

The victim of a mugging, it has been found, generally perceives the person who assaulted him to be larger and more menacing than he actually is. That is because the mind of the victim, out of fear, already has conjured up that vision while the incident is underway, overriding the images that are streaming in from the lens of his eyes. It is a time when reality – as seen through his eyes – has been relegated to the backseat by his mind. Similarly, people in an earthquake always believe that their harrowing experience lasted more than it actually did.

One can understand that human powers of observation become suspect under traumatic conditions. But the sad aspect is that, in many cases, our powers of observation are compromised for long periods in normal times. That is because we choose to see only what we wish to see and choose to hear only what we want to hear.

The fact is that even a standard question by someone will elicit different responses from us at different times, all depending on our mindset and how we wish to interpret the signal. For example, if you are extremely upset with your son for whatever reason, even if he was to genuinely ask how you are when you have just returned from a walk, you are likely to snap at him and perhaps tell him it was none of his business! That same question in the same tone would, at better times, be answered with a lot of warmth and affection.

Why the change in your response? The answer to that lies in yourself. It was your mental condition of being upset that triggered off a negative response in the earlier example. And that is so true in all our responses. They depend on our state of mind at that point of time.

It does not deserve any great insight to see the irrationality of such behaviour and decide that we must make amends and change such an attitude. Every response of ours must be independent of our mental make-up at that point in time and should be on its own merit.

While the benefits to the people we deal with are apparent, our response also has a lot of advantages for ourselves. For starters, we will not be misunderstood. Nor will we be manipulated. Because if the people around you know you are a person of moods, they can play the game to their own advantage as well!

39

Let Go of Fears

... begin by learning to accept yourself as you are.
Learn to be happy with all your irritations,
shortcomings, flaws and soon you will feel better.

WE ALL CONCEDE THAT WE NEED TO CHANGE OUR WAYS, OUR attitudes, our reactions and, indeed, our very matrix of existence. And we also acknowledge that the problems, and the solutions, all reside within us. You will also agree that unless we are all at peace within ourselves, and with ourselves, we cannot be at peace with the external world.

However, I have often discovered that the journey within does not take into consideration the externalities of the world we live in. It is relatively easy to retreat to the mountains and meditate, live a pious life and get rid of negative thoughts. It is far more difficult to stay in the crush of our cities, go to work in crowded buses and trains, tolerate intolerant bosses, handle demanding children and still find peace within ourselves. In such a situation, the aggravation usually comes from the externalities.

Against such a backdrop, I have noticed that many people who practise myriad self-help philosophies in sylvan retreats and find themselves in the lap of positivity, often lose their feel-good energies when they return to their homes where the real problems of life dwell. They form groups of similar practitioners, but the same feeling of being charged cannot be replicated.

I believe that it is so because in trying to reach inwards, we have not shed our externalities. And we can do so only by living them out entirely; and transcending them.

As I have mentioned before, a large part of our problems arises because we are full of fears: of making fools of ourselves, of being laughed at, of being found to be ignorant, of being unable to speak well, of being unable to dance well, of our past being discovered and so on.

Therefore, we are constantly unhappy with ourselves and project an image of ourselves that is not based on reality. Indeed, the higher up the socio-economic scale one goes, the more pretentious and serious – and laughable – the image becomes.

It is imperative to prick that image and begin by learning to accept yourself as you are. Learn to be happy with all your irritations, shortcomings, flaws and soon you will feel better. Laugh out loud, get angry, learn to dance … and trip … and lose your awkwardness. Relax and learn to be a fool … you will feel better.

Remember, the journey within can only begin from the outside. That is where the real problems lie …

40

Joy Is Uplifting

Perish the thought that you have to be sad to understand life. Life is something to feel good about. So live it with hope and courage. There are millions of people who have genuine reasons to be sad about. Be glad you are not one of them.

IN MAY 2011 I FLEW DOWN TO DELHI TO LAUNCH GAJRA KOTTARY'S book *Broken Melodies*. It is about a girl growing up in a broken family and going through trying times with nothing much to look forward to but hope and faith.

I agreed to be associated with the event as I felt the characters were well portrayed and the novel itself had a cinematic quality about it. It is a book that has some light relief and also many sombre tones. It is a classic case of the glass being half empty or half full, depending on what you wish to see. While some in the audience felt that tragedy is more real, not just in literature but also in life, others did not share this belief. The reason why I am referring to this event and discussion here is because I have strong views on the subject. I have seen too many lives getting twisted, in the belief that tragedy is real and everything else in life is unreal, to remain a bystander in such a discussion.

It is unfortunate that many young and talented people I knew, or heard about, have gone down the tube trying to self-flagellate themselves to feel the reality, which, they felt, was missing in their lives. Some have done it by cutting away from their comfortable backgrounds, others by embracing Bacchus and yet others by taking substances that give them a sense of altered reality.

Indeed, this is sad, and ironic, because there is no great virtue or truth to be discovered in plumbing sadness. Sadness, or shades of depression, makes us feel small. It reduces us and makes us shrink physically within ourselves.

Every one of you will realize the point I am making when you recall each time you shed a tear in the theatre or cinema hall, having seen a tragic moment. How you wiped a tear silently. You did not declaim your feelings to the world as sadness is a very private matter. It is uncommon to be publicly sad.

In contrast, do you ever remember yourself, or anyone else, laughing silently, or even trying to suppress it? Never. That is because laughter is loud, infectious and expansive. You never need to hide it. And in contrast to sadness, laughter is uplifting and gives you a feel-good sense at the end of it.

Every self-coaching programme, and I am not speaking of just laughter clubs that have mushroomed around the world, recommends humour. And, as even medical science now says, laughter is the best medicine. It is said that children laugh over three hundred times a day. But when we become adults, we feel the need to be serious, and so we laugh just about twenty times daily. No wonder we all look and feel constipated!

Perish the thought that you have to be sad to understand life. Life is something to feel good about. So live it with hope and courage. There are millions of people who have genuine reasons to be sad about. Be glad you are not one of them.

41

Discover Yourself

... discover yourself and follow your heart ....
Do not get despaired, but be inspired by life.
And look within yourself for that spark of inspiration.
Do not borrow it.

We can either be inspired, or be despaired, by life around us. In the days I grew up in Shimla, the majority had a middle-class, or a lower middle-class, existence. I am sure this growing-up experience is true for most of you as well. Wealth was only sensed, never openly seen. So, it was not too difficult to follow the Gandhian life. Indeed, there was little option.

Today, life is different. A new ostentatious attitude has taken over. It is now chic to flaunt your money, chase brands and live a hedonistic lifestyle. Even for the middle-class people, the slew of gadgets available in the market generates pressure on them to get acquisitive. So, we are continually assaulted by sights of great wealth, which creates a feeling of want, envy and inadequacy in many of us and it pushes us to emulate the 'success' we see all around.

That is how we get despaired by what we see. That is how we get pushed into adopting an attitude and emulating the 'successful' lifestyle of another person and also becoming someone else. And therein lie the seeds of much sadness in our lives.

It is imperative to understand ourselves and our limitations before we can assault the mountain of real success. It is in not understanding ourselves that we create a lot of chaos and unhappiness in us. If I believe that I ought to be a fashion designer to move with the swish set, but if I do not have any sense of colour, then I am only nurturing the seeds of unhappiness. If I aspire to become a film director to be in the glamour magazines, but if I do not have a sense of a story, then I should realize it is pack-up time for me. Even in less glamorous occupations, like being a culinary expert, if you cannot stand the heat in the kitchen, you do not have much of a future there.

The point is that the sooner we realize our limitations by holding a mirror to ourselves, the better it is for us. It is because we do not recognize ourselves, or fail to assess ourselves accurately, that the unhappiness blossoms in many of our lives.

I have come across scores of people who are still discovering themselves in their forties. It is indeed sad, for the forties is ideally a time when they should well have been on the road to reach the peak of their careers.

I am not for a moment saying that you should not push yourself to your limit. I am only saying that you should not chase another person's dream or success story. There are hundreds of engineers who have quit building machines and are making films, just as there are many doctors who are turning entrepreneurs. The point is to discover yourself and follow your heart – in time. Do not get despaired, but be inspired by life. And look within yourself for that spark of inspiration. Do not borrow it.

42

Value Your Relationships

We do not sustain what we have; yet,
if you talk to anyone around, you will realize that strained relationships
are the most common source of worry.

THERE ARE MANY MISCONCEPTIONS THAT MANY OF US LIVE BY. One of them is that we are all very rational people. Another is that we can live independently of each other. The latter idea is especially gaining ground in these days of consumerist gizmos and inventions such as the iPhone and the Internet, which have effectively estranged us from the physical presence of our friends, family and, indeed, society.

I had touched upon our growing social estrangement earlier also, but here I wish to write about such alienation and the findings of top flight behavioural study experts that relationships are the most important things in our lives. And that includes money too. Some have even quantified the value of happy relationships. According to one study, a happy husband–wife relationship is worth US $100,000, which works out to approximately Rs 50 lakh!

What are we doing about it? Are we aware of the state of our relationships with our spouses, our siblings, our sons and our daughters? Do we value the worth of our relationships? I do not think so. We, by and large, and it is natural as we are human, do not really worry overtly about nurturing relationships, until they go awry. And then, most often, we blame the other party for having transgressed limits and straining that bond. We do not sustain what we have; yet, if you talk to anyone around, you will realize that strained relationships are the most common source of worry.

A few weeks back, I met one of India's foremost management and life-skills counsellors who is perhaps the only professor to lecture at two national institutes of different disciplines. He told me that once he was conducting a workshop for senior bankers on some aspect of management. Within 15 minutes, all that the bankers were keen on discussing with him was a single topic: Relationships. Not leadership, not about motivating their workforce, but on how to nurture and mend relationships.

The point to note is that much as we are unaware, or perhaps do not care, it is relationships that we live for. We work, earn and struggle to give our families a better deal. Yet what is it all worth, if our families do not feel emotionally close to us?

I have seen patriarchs who are stern from the outside, but who break down when they realize their children do not love them. I have seen matriarchs who hate their daughters for perhaps marrying someone of their (daughters') choice. Yet the elder, in her innermost thoughts, cries when she recalls the bonds they shared during the daughter's growing up years.

Here, I would like to take an example from the Reiki masters who carefully evaluate each of their relationships every day, while expressing gratitude that the relationship is still alive. The principles of Reiki are: Just for Today, Don't Get Angry, Don't Worry, Be Grateful, Work Hard and Be Kind to Others.

That is the kernel of The Change Within …

43

Different Strokes for Different Folks

At a very basic level it has been established that even the optimal dosage of a formulation varies for men and women. So we need different strokes for different folks.

THE BEAUTY OF LIFE IS THAT WE ALL FEEL THAT WE ARE ALIKE, yet we are so different from each other. While it may be a nice warm feeling to feel kinship with the rest of humankind, to feel that we are one, it is sometimes necessary to realize that we are all different in many ways. For example, the bane of many life-coaching programmes is to believe in the approach that one size fits all. Nothing can be further from the truth.

That is why you keep meeting people who have been trying out different programmes. Some benefit from one type and some from another. But, in the process, many lose faith in being able to help themselves through such programmes as they feel they are unable to change.

What we should recognize is the fact that everyone on this planet is unique; we are all made differently. And, this is a proven genetic truth. Similarly, we all have our different problems, so one cure cannot treat us all. Medical science itself has now come to recognize that different medications act differently on different people. At a very basic level, it has been established that even the optimal dosage of a formulation varies for men and women. So we need different strokes for different folks.

Many people will immediately realize this fundamental truth by comparing life-coaching programmes to dieting. There are so many dieting regimens around but, as is very evident, not every diet programme works for everyone. Each person needs a different eating plan and even that plan may change as time goes by. So how does one choose a plan that fits in with one's needs?

The answer lies largely in your own hands and you should begin by looking at yourself in the mirror, metaphorically speaking. Analyse what kind of a person you are in terms of your characteristics and what are your essential problem areas. And then compare the methods that different programmes offer. If you have an angry disposition with problems of anger management, you may perhaps require a course on how to release that pent-up anger. Later, you need to also delve into what makes you angry and then learn how not to get affected by such triggers. A programme of meditation, of quietening your restless insides, will definitely help you.

But the same course will not be of much help to a person with a 'shrinking violet' type of personality. That person needs something else that will instil confidence in him or her and erase the constant fears of doubt that plague him or her on whether or not he or she will be able to rise to the occasion. For him or her, the journey within, of quiet contemplation, will not help as much as exercises in a group that will enable him or her to come out of his or her 'shell'.

So look at yourself, and decide what you are and what could suit your purpose, before you jump headlong into programmes that may not be cut out for you.

44

Let Go of Apron Strings

... success is not for the faint-hearted.
Get out of your comfort zone, stop clinging to the familiar
and steel yourself for the unexpected.
Because that is the only road to being aware ... and alive.

We all love to cling to people, things, places and associations. That is certainly an endearing trait and many nice terms are used to describe it, such as being sentimental. It is indeed nice to be even a sentimental fool, as the phrase goes; it is much better than being unsentimental and bordering on the unemotional. However, it is also true that many of our problems arise because we tend to cling to things for too long, well past their expiry dates.

Let us examine even the most primal relationship, that of a mother and her child. It is a very crucial bond because no child can ever hope to survive without the mother in the early stages of his or her life. It is not just the need of nourishment, but the child also needs constant warmth, care and hugs to survive, both physically and emotionally. Studies of infants without mothers – and in the care of the best European orphanages – have shown that, despite the finest nourishment, the mortality rate was much higher than infants with their mothers. The critical missing input was body warmth and hugs, it was concluded.

But even this relationship has an expiry date. When the child grows into an adult, the apron strings must be gradually loosened or we have a mama's boy and a papa's girl. Parents must gently give up controlling their children's lives and encourage them to take their own decisions. Overdependence on parents results in a stifled personality and emotional adjustment issues for the young adults. It leads to problems initially for their spouses and then for their families. So, the key to nipping such issues in the bud is for parents to stop clinging to their children when they are in their early teens.

There are other things we sometimes needlessly cling on to, such as our job when we are clearly unhappy with it and relationships that we have outgrown. I have noticed that many times people hang on to a job that does not excite them. Maybe they have outgrown it, or maybe their bosses are having a mid-life crisis. Whatever be the reason, if the very prospect of going to work every morning triggers a depressive thought, then it is time to scout around for another job and move on. There is no point in living in misery. What goes for jobs also goes for some relationships that are not working out. Moving on is progress, it is not defeat.

Why do many of us cling to people or things? It is because we like to hang on to the familiar and are involuntarily scared of change. And that unwillingness grows stronger as we grow older with each passing year. Given a choice, we want to go to familiar places and be met by familiar people. But success is not for the faint-hearted. Get out of your comfort zone, stop clinging to the familiar and steel yourself for the unexpected. Because that is the only road to being aware … and alive.

45

In Failure Lies Success

It is the willingness to learn from our reverses that is the critical difference between successful people and the not-so-successful ones.

Earlier I touched briefly on the subject of coping with failure. Every May-June when results of the schools' boards, and of examinations for entry to professional courses, are announced, we see huge disappointments and even suicides by some students who did not make it. I think it is time for a larger discussion. The basic point I wish to get across is that we ought to change our perceptions of failure. Do not view failure as permanent; it is temporary. Do not call it failure; call it a reverse, or a setback, if you will. Do not think of a reverse negatively; think of it also positively in terms of the lessons it can teach you.

And if you manage to successfully view a failure as a reverse, you will never think of it as an end-of-the-road situation. Instead, you will view it as a bend in the road, which could lead on to broader avenues.

As teenagers, your reverses, at this time of the year at least, are largely of the academic kind. To you – and more importantly to your parents – I would like to pose one question. Think of any topper in any endeavour, be it sports or painting or in business or in politics or in the performing arts. Was that person a topper in studies? The answer, most definitely, is a NO. So, if the best are not really academic successes, a reverse can never really be a closed chapter in your career.

Let me give you a very concrete example, which sounds incredible, but which can be checked in a jiffy in these days of the Internet. Without argument, the greatest scientist of the last century, whose abstruse theories are still being tested, was Albert Einstein. And do you know that he failed in his first attempt at the entrance examination for admission to the famed Swiss Federal Institute of Technology at Zurich the age of 16? Yet he landed up with the Nobel Prize …

Similarly, you can search for the legendary story of Robert de Bruce, the legendary king of Scotland, who was inspired by a spider, after failing to dislodge the British from his country in six battles. He succeeded in his seventh attempt.

Reverses may be linked with academics in our competitive milieu, but as we all realize, reverses will occur in every field: in our finances, our occupation, our relationships and many more. It is therefore imperative that we learn to analyse our reverses and never fear them.

Every decision that we take has a 50 per cent chance of success; and an equal chance of failure. Yet we all have to take decisions. So, we must accept that the road to success will always be littered with mistakes and reverses. It is the willingness to learn from our reverses that is the critical difference between successful people and the not-so-successful ones.

So, do not be terrified of failure, or reverses. Often, as in the cases of Einstein and King Robert, in failure lies the seed of success. As they say: 'Greatness lies not in never falling, but in rising every time we fall.'

46

Allow Friendship Time and Space

... keep it [friendship] light. Value it and do not
expect too much from your friends;
the weight of your expectations can sometimes break it up.
Over the years, let your friendship find its own weight and level.

'TELL ME WHO YOUR FRIENDS ARE AND I WILL TELL YOU WHAT you are', goes an old saying. Not without reason, as friendship is a relationship that has the strongest, and also the frailest, of bonds.

If there many incredible stories of loyalty that are centred around this relationship, there are perhaps twice as many that end up in disappointment. If people have given up kingdoms for friendship, they have also betrayed friends for the proverbial thirty pieces of silver. And that is why friendship remains among the most fascinating of relationships.

Of course, there are different types of friends and friendships. I am not referring to links that are formed at the workplace or in social circles or in the neighbourhood. These associations are conveniently geographic in nature and change when we move out of our jobs or localities. The relationships I am referring to are ones forged during the early years, in an age of trust and innocence, and much before one is exposed to wiles, greed and commerce.

It is not that friendship is an easy relationship; indeed, there are too few friendships that last through the decades, through all the ups and downs that life bestows on us.

Why do friendships not always last? The reasons may be varied but they mostly centre on a sense of inequality creeping into the relationship and one party putting less store by it than the other. As a rule, people find it much easier to remain friends when both continually remain on the same socio-economic level than if one has a drastic upswing in fortune, leading to disparity.

Generally, people do not like to carry the baggage from their modest days when they are swirling in heady success. Sadly, they are unaware of their loss. In contrast, I am fortunate to have maintained my close and abiding friendship with Vijay Sehgal from my school days in Shimla, even though we are separated by cities, interests and professions. And I think the gain has been mine as Vijay, sometimes my staunchest critic, has always helped in keeping me linked with reality. That is the advantage of a real friendship.

There is another reason why friendships go kaput over time.

And that is because of great expectations from one side, which are not reciprocated by the other. Over time, this sense of inequality in expectations creates a chasm that becomes unbridgeable. I know of several people who would give their right arm for their friends, but when their buddies are more circumspect about their loyalties, fissures start appearing. I am not judging on the basis of the reasons for people being prudent; perhaps circumstances have changed, new priorities such as marriage and children may have crept in. But such changes need to be factored in.

My advice to all young friends is to keep it light. Value it and do not expect too much from your friends; the weight of your expectations can sometimes break it up. Over the years, let your friendship find its own weight and level.

47

Adaptability to Change

Some view change as a learning experience and take it as a challenge; almost like learning a new hobby. Others feel threatened by it; as if it is a new technology that has to be harnessed. Yet others do not feel that they need to change at all.

CHANGE MAY BE A POPULAR MANTRA, BUT WE ALL HAVE different responses to change. Even among men and women. Some view change as a learning experience and take it as a challenge; almost like learning a new hobby. Others feel threatened by it; as if it is a new technology that has to be harnessed. Yet others do not feel that they need to change at all. If you look at it from another perspective, some of us know what our shortcomings are. Many do not. And the sad part is, that despite guidance, the rest are not prepared to accept that they have certain flaws in their attitudes, which need to be corrected.

The rueful fact is that you cannot change a person, in whichever aspect we are talking about, unless that person is prepared to accept his or her deficiency and then s/he tries to change. There is empirical evidence that women, especially in the Indian milieu, are more keen to seek a change in their lives and are hence amenable to change. Part of the reason I believe is that girls, from a young age, are taught to think of the sensitivities of others in their families, and consider themselves last. In orthodox families, they are even trained how to look after their future in-laws and gain acceptance in their husband's home. Again, after marriage, a girl has to live with a totally new set of relatives and learn to cope with, and adapt to, her circumstances. No such adaptability is ever demanded from males, and therefore, predictably, they are more resistant to change.

I have known several people who have gone through their entire adulthood not apologizing to anyone as they resolutely believe that they have never committed an error in their lives! And in the course of their distorted realities, they wreak untold havoc and misery on their near and dear ones. If there are any reasons why such people have remained non-achievers, rather than examine their lapses, they blithely palm off the blame on their parents, later their spouses and finally even their children. Yes, such people are almost always men!

This is not to say that men are inferior; it is just that they are more resistant to change than women. The truth is that women's brains are wired 30 per cent more efficiently in terms of neural connections between the two hemispheres, which makes them better at multitasking, seeing the larger picture of life more easily and thinking of the long term; all of which make them ideal mothers and nurturers. Men, as they have less information flow between the hemispheres, in turn have a more compartmentalized approach to life and think more of the here-and-now issues and less of the long term.

Rather than debating the merits of the brains of the sexes, it would be best to concentrate on why we are what we are. Men and women must understand each other's imperatives and realize why some are more adaptable to change and why some others are not.

48

Never Put Off till Tomorrow What You Can Do Today

It is a sense of lethargy that overcomes many of us.
Delays pile up beyond days, and the days then turn into months.
And before long we pass the anniversary of our big idea.

ASK YOUR FRIENDS WHAT IS THE GREATEST LABOUR-SAVING device ever invented and you will get varied answers. Men may believe that it is the automobile, the computer, or maybe a robot.

Women may think it is the washing machine or plumbing, which brings water into your homes. No, it is none of these; it is the word 'tomorrow'. The word is a wonderful excuse for putting off things and it is also an excuse for not delivering. Sadly, it is also the reason for failures that have bedevilled the lives of many people who have not been able to leverage their potential.

In my line, I have come across many talented people who had

wonderful ideas. But they just did not execute them and, before long, someone else walked away with the honours. Sometime back, for example, I met a talented stand-up comedian from Los Angeles who had come up with a wonderful concept for a comedy television series. But he sat on it for six months. Someone else wrote it out and presented it to the channel and it is now a top-ranking television show in the US. He is ruing his lethargy now.

If you analyse the situation, the problem with our tomorrows is the gap between an idea and its execution. It is a sense of lethargy that overcomes many of us. Delays pile up beyond days, and the days then turn into months. And before long we pass the anniversary of our big idea.

Many of us have fallen in this gap, but we learn our lessons. Unfortunately, some still do not. This problem is particularly true among teenagers who have a habit of chilling out and believe that their parents are killjoys for expecting things to be done in time. They grow out of this habit when they join the mainstream of the working class, because in an office situation, delays are not condoned beyond a point.

But it is largely the creative fields that are mainly seized with this problem, as there are no deadlines when you are alone. You will find many writers working endlessly on scripts as you will find many composers thinking of that great tune.

And the problem is that they do not push themselves to their limits. In my own case, I am frequently down with colds, viral fever and a bad throat due to my constant travelling. Yet I push myself to the very edge and report on the sets every time, and on time. I never make excuses and keep my commitments, much to the amazement of my manager. I am not alone in my profession; there are others too who are very professional. And that is the reason why they are successful.

So take your commitment seriously and do not procrastinate. Hold review meetings with yourself every night and analyse if the time you spent that day could have been more fruitfully spent. And finally, be a hard taskmaster on yourself. Because you will gain to benefit the most from the exercise.

49

Early Lessons in Life Create Lasting Impressions

Modern research shows that emotions and feelings can be formed before we are even born! All our emotions are stored in the limbic portion of the brain, which is often referred to as our 'emotional' brain.

WHAT HAS INDIA'S EPIC MAHABHARATA GOT TO DO WITH cutting-edge research into the human brain? The link is how it is difficult to forget our early brain inputs!

Modern research shows that emotions and feelings can be formed before we are even born! All our emotions are stored in the limbic portion of the brain, which is often referred to as our 'emotional' brain. Of particular interest is one section of our emotional brain, the seat of most of our feelings, called the amygdala. The amazing thing about the amygdala is that it becomes functional long before birth. It has been found that it is processing and, more importantly, storing feelings and emotions, even at the pre-birth stage.

To most of us Indians, this knowledge of the brain's inputs being active even in the pre-birth phase is not surprising as we are aware of the story of Arjuna, his son Abhimanyu and the Chakravyuha. In the Mahabharata, the unborn Abhimanyu learnt how to break into the deadly battle formation of the Chakravyuha when Arjuna was explaining it to his pregnant wife. But as Arjuna was called away by Lord Krishna and could not complete the explanation, Abhimanyu did not learn the secret of getting out of the Chakravyuha. Tragically, his lack of knowledge later cost him his life.

Right now, many pregnant mothers in Europe are placing audio headphones on their bellies and feeding their unborn children language lessons in the hope that the little ones will be multilingual when they are born! But more seriously, the point is that if it is difficult to forget the lessons picked up so early in life, it is equally difficult to unlearn negative emotions such as anger, sadness, loneliness, and many others, which are formed at the same time. They manifest themselves as blockages in our later life and prevent us from leveraging our potential.

To help clear such blockages, I wish to share with you an exercise I have recommended often. Sit down comfortably, close your eyes and breathe deeply and evenly. Think of your current placement, the room you are in and your body and go in deeper, into your very lungs, as you inhale and exhale. Then go back in time ten years. Where are you now? Familiarize yourself with your surroundings. Wait for a while ... maybe you are playing with your college mates. Go back in time another 10 years ... where are you now ... in school? Can you see your playground, your classmates? Remember the pranks you used to play on them? Relax and familiarize yourself again. Now go back another ten years to when you were five years old perhaps. Familiarize yourself again.

Now go back to the time, for the last time, when you were in your mother's womb. The light is soft ... you are floating securely in tepid waters. You are serene. After enjoying this sensation for some time, now imagine slowly that you are being born ... again ... afresh ... without fears, anger or stress.

Do this slowly, gently, and you will be able to gradually erase many of the negative blockages that constrict you.

50

Coping with Loss and Death

There are many responses that I have encountered to sudden deaths. Some are too numbed to react. Others react with a quiet dignity. Yet others break down inconsolably. There are no hard-and-fast rules, just as there is nothing that is correct or incorrect in grief.

SUDDEN DEATH WAS UPON OUR PUBLIC CONSCIOUSNESS AGAIN with the bomb blasts in Mumbai on 13 July 2011. And sudden bereavement is among the hardest losses to cope with as there are both an air of suddenness and a sense of finality to it. One accepts fate more easily if an aged relative who has been ailing for long has passed away. Death is inevitable and expected in such cases. But it is infinitely more difficult when the sequence of life and living is upturned; when a father carries his son to the pyre or grave, instead of the other way around.

When death comes, it is very difficult to console the near and dear ones. Words are meaningless and can only offer some solace, but not beyond a point. Ultimately, the journey is one of loss and aloneness for the ones who are bereaved. Only a wife can understand the loss of her spouse who has left her widowed, suddenly. Only a mother can understand the anguish of losing her firstborn, however imperfect s/he may have been in life.

There are many responses that I have encountered to sudden deaths. Some are too numbed to react. Others react with a quiet dignity. Yet others break down inconsolably. There are no hard-and-fast rules, just as there is nothing that is correct or incorrect in grief. There are similarly many ways of coping with grief. Many people do not wish to be disturbed; many others go into depression.

Perhaps the finest example of coping with the grief of sudden death, which I have seen, concerns the family of the Mahajans near Pune who lost their son Maitreyi in a tragic motorbike accident some years ago, when he was barely 22. Maitreyi always wanted to become a biker and was a sketch artist of some merit. His scrapbook was full of messages like 'I Love to Ride', with sketches of bikes on wings. Ironically, he had also worked on a colourful graphic, 'Riders Don't Die'. Predictably, the Mahajans were shattered with his death. But Maitreyi's parents, Vidhur and Aparna, have slowly picked up the pieces of their tragedy and have now transcended it. I saw a calm resolve in them when I visited them recently. Vidhur has written a book in Marathi on his son and the tragedy titled *Maitrey Jivachi*, which translates as 'friends for life', to help him, and the family, overcome the loss.

I feel a kinship with such sudden death cases as my first memorable role was that of a retired school master, B. B. Pradhan, in *Saraansh*, a man who helps his wife cope with the death of their only child in the US. To me, the only way out when the feeling of loss subsides is to understand and appreciate that the Maitreyis of this world did live life fully for 22 years. For his parents and friends, it was a wonderful opportunity to have lived with him during that time. And that opportunity is infinitely better, than if he had not been with them at all.

Postscript

THIS IS A BOOK THAT SHOWCASES THE GRAPH OF MY LIFE. It encapsulates the life I have lived and experienced; not about life as gleaned from a book. It is about my journey, my outlook towards everything, including failure and success. And contradictory to what many people believe, it is in fact easier to deal with failure than with success.

When I look back and see how I survived and kept my sanity through the toughest times of my life, I can attribute it to just one thing. That would be my attitude. It is the attitude of never giving up on hope. I believed, and I still do, that the next breakthrough is always just around the corner. I think hope is the single most powerful source of sustenance for anyone. And if hope is lost, everything is lost.

Through my faith in hope, I essentially came to believe in myself. Very often, especially when one is going through difficult days, it is easy to fall prey to self-doubts and be swayed momentarily by other people's advice. While I am not saying that one should not recalibrate one's energies or focus, it is imperative never to lose sight of one's objective. Persistence and hard work are virtues that pay off in the long run, not vacillating whether to be, or not to be.

Yet, we must learn to change, because change is the mantra of nature. We have to shed some old habits and pick up new ones along the journey of life. Technically, I am the same person I was before I became an actor. I may seem unchanged on the surface. But a lot has changed within me. I still have the fire of hope, but it has been tempered with age and experience.

When I speak of change, I am not advocating that we abandon all that we have stood for all through our lives. While we have to remain steadfast to certain aspects like values, we must have the wisdom to accept the inevitability of change, just as we must accept the changing seasons.

Some of you may think that there is a contradiction between remaining steadfast and accepting change. If you have read the book closely, you will realize that life is full of contradictions. Our strengths also become our weaknesses. When we are young, we think of life, and people, as clear-cut blacks and whites. Only later do we realize that life is just shades of grey. And the grey becomes what we wish to make out of it.

During the worst phase of my life, when I hit rock bottom financially, I decided to do a play in order to earn some money. It was an autobiographical play that I did out of necessity. I thought of looking at the failures of my life in a different light; in a humorous way. The audiences loved *Kuchh Bhi Ho Sakta Hai* for the message of hope it delivered. And while watching them, I suddenly realized that I had an epiphany – I was no longer afraid of failure ...

My play *Kuchh Bhi Ho Sakta Hai* is my autobiography – the most creative product of my life, which came along only because I needed to survive. This book is a firsthand account of what I have learned throughout my life and I won't be exaggerating when I say that my failures have helped me create the two most beautiful extensions of myself – my acting school Actor Prepares and my play. Today, I have completed over 225 shows of my play and it has become an extension of my philosophy. And I want to take that philosophy far and wide to reach as many people as possible, so that they too may share my life-changing truths and benefit from my experiences.

That is why I will soon be launching *Kuchh Bhi Ho Sakta Hai* as a life-coaching programme. It will contain the essence of life and living. And it could be the best thing that might happen to you yet because, as I always say, the best book about life is life itself!

Acknowledgements

MANY YEARS HAVE GONE INTO THE CRAFTING OF THIS BOOK, which, essentially, is about coping with life and living. It could not have been possible without the experiences of meeting and learning from the many people I have encountered over the years.

I have always believed, and this belief has now been attested by research, that our emotional construct in life gets embedded in our childhood. For the rest of our lives we merely polish what is within us. I therefore wish to thank my parents: my father Pushkarnath and my mother Dulari for giving me a wonderful emotional base which I could build upon. My father, especially, always radiated positivity; he is an ordinary man, but the more I have seen of life, the more I realize that in being ordinary, he is extraordinary. During those formative years, I also appreciated the roles of my younger brother Raju, a loyalist, and of my closest friend Vijay Sehgal, who continues to remain my benchmark of simplicity even now.

Every writing endeavour silently takes its toll on the ones who are close to the author. In this case it is my wife Kirron whose abiding faith in me has been the bedrock for many of my thoughts that run through this compendium. Then there is the late Sister Maria Dolores of the Dilkhush Special School, a school in Mumbai for children who are mentally challenged. In a world filled with distrust, she taught me the importance of trusting strangers. I cannot forget that lesson!

While I owe a debt of gratitude to everyone I met, and got inspired by, during the writing of this book, this volume would not have been possible without the timely support and help of the publishers of the *Deccan Chronicle* and A. T. Jayanti, its chief editor. I am grateful to Mahesh Bhatt for giving me my first break in *Saraansh* (1984), without which I would not be what I am today, and also to Pritish Nandy, who taught me how to be fearless.

A special word of thanks to Sailesh Kottary for giving clarity to my thoughts. My thanks to the photographers, Taarini Chopra, Jesse Robertson, Raghav Khattar and Prem Kumar Singh, for the beautiful photographs included in this book and to Atul Kasbekar for the cover picture. How does one thank Noni Chawla? He placed at my disposal his entire bank of thousands of photographs with a simple message: 'Choose whatever you want to. It's all yours.' My thanks also to Aeshna Roy for designing the book so elegantly and to K. J. Ravinder for fine-tuning the text.

Finally, I must confess that I had no doubt in my mind that it would be my old friend Ashok Chopra who would publish this book. The result is there for you to see!